listening
helping
learning

CORE COMPETENCIES OF
PROCESS CONSULTING

listening helping learning

In this important book the reader will find not only a clear account of what Process Consulting is, as distinct from many other kinds of organizational consulting, but also the relevant skills needed for helpers of all kinds—if they are to deliver real help to their Clients. Helping is itself a complex human relationship, and to deliver it competently as Process Consultants therefore requires not only the intention to help but also the skills described in this book.

    —Edgar H. Schein

    Professor Emeritus, MIT Sloan School of Management

    Author with Peter Schein, *Humble Inquiry*, (rev.ed. 2021),

    Humble Leadership (2018), *Humble Consulting* (2016)

What I love most about Mark L. Vincent is his capacity to humanize process—to apply systematic principles to the real conversations we are already having. There is approachable depth here. The depth is necessary because you can't shortcut wisdom and discernment as a consultant or as a person, but it must be easily consumable. Whether you are a parent or a president, *Listening, Helping, Learning* is deep education in the best thinking in Process Consulting that is written for the experts—and for the rest of us.

    —Dr. Rob McKenna

    CEO, WiLD Leaders

    Founder, The WiLD Foundation

In my decades of consulting work, I've found that the most difficult truths to unearth are usually the most obvious ones. That's why I love to draw: drawing forces the obvious to come to the surface. In this wonderful book, Mark and Kim do the same: they gently knock us on the head with the reminder that the heart of Process Consulting is people. The better we listen, the more we can learn. The better we see, the more we can help. Read this book and remember how to listen and to see.

    —Dan Roam

    Author, *The Back of the Napkin, Draw to Win,* and *The Pop-Up Pitch*

MARK L. VINCENT

Foreword by Kim Stezala

listening
helping
learning

CORE COMPETENCIES OF
PROCESS CONSULTING

TENTH POWER

ELGIN, IL • TYLER, TX

www.tenthpowerpublishing.com

Copyright © 2022 by Design Group International

www.societyforprocessconsulting.com

All rights reserved. No part of this book may be reproduced without permission from the author, except by a reviewer quoting brief passages in a review; nor may any part of this book be reproduced, stored in a retrieval system or copied by mechanical photocopying, recording or other means without written permission from the author.

Scriptures taken from the Holy Bible, New International Version®, NIV®. Copyright © 1973, 1978, 1984, 2011 by Biblica, Inc.™ Used by permission of Zondervan. All rights reserved worldwide. www.zondervan.com The "NIV" and "New International Version" are trademarks registered in the United States Patent and Trademark Office by Biblica, Inc.™

Cover and interior design by LTD2

Hardcover ISBN: 978-1-938840-52-4
e-book ISBN: 978-1-938840-53-1

10 9 8 7 6 5 4 3 2 1

To all who seek first to listen, then to understand.
May what you read here call to you and feed you.
May it bring you face to face with an opportunity to become more fully human.
May it find its way into the organizations you serve so
others not yet born may live fulfilling lives also.

CONTENTS

Foreword	11
Introduction	17
An Opening Chapter: WWWWWH	23

LISTENING

The First Core Competency—Listening Actively and Comprehensively	31
The Second Core Competency—Listening Conceptually and Contextually	47
The Third Core Competency—Listening Architecturally	63
The Fourth Core Competency—Listening Adaptively	79

HELPING

The Fifth Core Competency—Helping: Client-Centered	95
The Sixth Core Competency—Helping: Client-Owned and Client-Inspired	115
The Seventh Core Competency—Helping: Client-Specific	129
The Eighth Core Competency—Helping: Client Success	147

LEARNING

The Ninth Core Competency—Learning in Partnership	161
The Tenth Core Competency—Learning toward Wisdom	177
The Eleventh Core Competency—Learning to Exchange	193
The Twelfth Core Competency—Learning toward Posterity	211

A Final Word	225
End Notes	227
Contributors	233
About the Author	239
Acknowledgments	241
Additional Resources	243

Foreword

THE HISTORY OF THE TWELVE CORE COMPETENCIES

The Twelve Core Competencies were created as a practical tool and guide to establish indicators of proficiency in Process Consulting, a field originally described by the prolific Edgar Schein. Many of this book's contributors are devotees of Schein and his works, including *Process Consultation, Process Consultation Revisited, Humble Inquiry,* and *Humble Consulting.* His writings describe the traits and functions of a Process Consultant in detail, but they do not define the necessary *competencies* of that Process Consultant; this is the gap we seek to fill with our addition to the Process Consulting canon.

These Twelve Core Competencies were born out of the three core values of Design Group International (DGI), the Community of Practice (COP) where I serve as a Senior Design Partner. DGI's core values are Listening, Helping, and Learning, and that *-ing* suffix is vital in conveying the active nature of our collaborative and iterative work. Every member of DGI practices Process Consulting, and Schein's works are included in the onboarding for our new members for that reason.

As Design Group International grew and expanded to include the Society for Process Consulting, which offers in-depth courses and certifications in Process Consulting, we realized the need to further develop the foundation laid by Schein into something even more practical and definitive. As evangelists of what we earnestly believe to be a superior form of consulting, and while honoring the legacy of Schein as the "godfather" of Process Consulting, we worked through multiple iterations to thoroughly identify the field's essential competencies. Naturally, the next step was to document them thoroughly, which led to the development of this book.

THE TWELVE CORE COMPETENCIES OF PROCESS CONSULTING

Listening Actively and Comprehensively
Listening Conceptually and Contextually
Listening Architecturally
Listening Adaptively

Helping: Client-Centered
Helping: Client-Owned and Client-Inspired
Helping: Client-Specific
Helping: Client Success

Learning in Partnership
Learning toward Wisdom
Learning to Exchange
Learning toward Posterity

The Twelve Core Competencies were vetted in the field by Process Consultants through the DGI COP and the Society for Process Consulting's Standards and Ethics Committee. They were subject to thorough debate, detailed word-smithing, and final approval by the seasoned and innovative members of our COP. Even so, they are not set in stone, and we fully expect them to evolve as the field evolves. We will continue scanning the environment, adapting, and updating the Competencies as this domain of consulting grows.

The Twelve Core Competencies explored throughout this book are taught in all the Society's courses, with members earning certification to represent their level of competency as sufficient, proficient, or excellent. However, even at the highest rung on the ladder, we know that there is always room for more growth! As Process Consultants, we approach learning and growth as lifelong endeavors.

WHAT WE HOPE TO ACHIEVE

With this book, written by Process Consultants for Process Consultants, we seek to accelerate learning in organizational development by providing hands-on lessons and examples from the field of Process Consulting. Our intention is to bridge academia with practical examples and connections to the real world, inspiring our readers toward continual learning and development of their craft. We hope to stimulate conversation and to build community, particularly for individuals who seek to approach consulting in a different way, but who may not have found the language to talk about what that difference is until discovering this community.

Even more broadly, we want to build up the movement against consulting that takes the form of *Let me just give you the answer*. We are not "Pez dispenser" product-focused consultants, popping out solutions at the press of a button.

We want to show another, better way of consulting in response to the deep, deep need that exists in today's world for adaptive and iterative approaches. The COVID-19 pandemic exposed this need to a glaring degree, as organizations that failed to evolve failed to survive. This book is in part for the rising generation of consultants who lived through that whirlwind, and who can see more clearly than ever the need to move away from transactional consulting in the direction of relational and transformational consulting.

We'll take a moment here to acknowledge that what we are doing is not new. Throughout history, humans have been solving problems by asking good questions. Think of the Socratic method of learning, with its emphasis on dialogue, iteration, and inquiry. As Process Consultants who walk alongside Clients (and yes, the capitalization of Client is intentional and will be explained in the Introduction) as guides and thought partners, rather than experts with quick answers that serve as temporary solutions, we know that our methods are only a continuation of the human tendencies to question, listen, learn, and build. With the publication of this book, we simply hope to disseminate this ancient approach in a practical, digestible, and modern form, and to unleash the power of this methodology, as it is manifested in Process Consulting, across the world.

THE WRITER: MARK L. VINCENT

Spouses Mark L. Vincent and Lorie Vincent co-founded Design Group International in 2000. Two decades later, the company remains a community of Process Consultants committed to a "better way" of consulting, one that honors the Client first rather than a product or solution. After Lorie's passing in 2015, Mark continued to grow the company and was instrumental in the launch of the Society for Process Consulting, where he teaches foundational courses for those seeking a professional credential. Mark also founded Maestro-level leaders, a peer-based leadership journey for highly developed executives. With more than 35 years of experience pioneering a variety of approaches to executive leadership and organizational capacity-building, Mark has authored previous books (including *A Christian View of Money*) and co-hosts the *Third Turn Podcast*.

Mark is a consummate innovator and writer whose work and reflections sparked the formation of the Twelve Core Competencies. A pioneer upholding the field, Mark's commitment to fostering next generations of Process Consultants propels the goals of this book: to build the platform, to pass on generational wisdom, and to continuously grow, respond, and improve.

FOREWORD: THE HISTORY OF THE TWELVE CORE COMPETENCIES

A WIDE VARIETY OF CASE STUDIES: OUR INTENTION

This book does not seek to capture one person's story. Rather, it is a collection of case studies, two for each of the competencies, written by distinguished Process Consultants. The case studies come from large and small businesses, non-profits, associational groups, ministry settings, and education. Many of our contributors live or work internationally, and no two bring the exact same perspective or context to the exploration of their competency of focus.

A complete list of these contributors can be found at the end of the book.

The strength of Process Consulting is that, at its core, it is meant to be cross cultural, multigenerational, and able to adapt to an infinite number of contexts. Even more than that, it is meant to be not only *inclusive*, which implies that we are inviting others into a closed space, but *expansive*, which implies that the walls can be broken down entirely! With a *highly competent* Process Consultant at the helm (and that piece, of course, is where this book comes in), Process Consulting can work in thousands of organizational settings, business disciplines, and professional sectors.

The skills and competencies we explore in these pages are not meant only for formal, external consultants, but also for those who fill consultative roles internally: C-Suite executives, corporate boards, program managers, department managers, strategy managers, and more. Accordingly, these internal roles are represented in several of the case studies.

Finally, you will notice that these case studies do not contain any talk of resolution. Each one is left open-ended, allowing the scenarios to develop in your mind and nudging you toward discussion with others. Read on and dig into these case studies as stories to remember and serve as guideposts.

—Kim Stezala
CEO, the Society for Process Consulting

INTRODUCTION

Moving beyond raw data toward wisdom is a journey. Much gets discarded or distilled along the way:

- We sift raw *data* so it can be shared as *information*.
- *Information* is then rendered and sequenced to pass along to others as *knowledge*.
- *Knowledge* successfully and repeatedly applied in a variety of contexts becomes recognized *expertise*.
- *Expertise* analyzed, broken down, put back together, combined with other expertise, and then folded into an intuitive and non-anxious, creative forward leap is one way we recognize *wisdom*.

The journey from mere advising to the deeper wisdom of Process Consulting follows a similar path:

- Advising in general is dispensing perspective whether it is useful or not. Someone has a data point, and they choose to share it. *An Advisor tells.*
- Intellectual Property tends to be this same perspective organized for publication and dissemination, what increasingly gets labeled as *content*. Content is either for general consumption, available for

a consumer's purchase, or is an add-on resource tied to a Client engagement. *An Expert sells.*

- Subject Matter Expertise, what we might also describe as contracting or serving as a vendor, is that same Intellectual Property applied with a specific Client and for that Client's context. *A Subject Matter Expert sells and tells.*

- Consulting connects multiple lines of subject matter expertise to address a Client's unique need for change, often at a technical level. The Consultant chooses between tools, assessments, or other processes to determine what the Client needs to do. *Consultants sell, assess, tell, then sell again.*

- Process Consulting joins with the Client in not knowing what to do exactly, especially as the Client faces adaptive and/or complex change. The Process Consultant brings a non-anxious curiosity alongside the Client to design the steps (the process) they will follow to go from where they believe they are to where they want to be. The Process Consultant asks, *What do you need to do?* followed by *What are you willing to do? In partnership with the Client, the Process Consultant listens, then helps, and then learns* (see Fig.1).

WHAT	WHO	HOW
Data	Advisor	Filters
Information	Intellectual Property/Content Creator	Organizes
Knowledge	Subject Matter Expert	Specializes
Expertise	Consultant	Applies
Wisdom	Process Consultant	Innovates Together

Figure 1

INTRODUCTION

As our new millennium began, a Community of Practice with Process Consulting at its center came to life.[1] Out of this Community of Practice the Society for Process Consulting was born, establishing standards, ethics, and the Twelve Core Competencies for the Process Consulting profession.

The Twelve Core Competencies fall into three categories: Listening, Helping, and Learning. Each category includes four competencies. The Twelve Core Competencies are not completely distinct from each other. Rather, they overlap, fold into each other, and can sometimes prove to be reinforcing and inseparable. We often use the metaphor of Russian nesting dolls (Fig. 2) in pointing to this overlapping reinforcement. By the time reflective readers turn the last page of this book, they will be more able to recognize a competency, more prepared to put that competency to use, and more appreciative of how, together, these competencies reflect the whole of a well-developed Process Consulting practice.

In 2020, a curriculum for introducing and developing these competencies became available through the Society for Process Consulting.[2] The first participants who completed the course kept describing a personal and professional transformational experience. They described being unwound and then rewound, unformed and reformed.

Many found themselves repeatedly returning to the course material to orient themselves when preparing to work with a new Client or to self-evaluate once a Client engagement ended. Several participants asked us to publish the course material as a book to use and share with others—so now you hold it in your hands.

This book comes to you with a simple structure. After an opening chapter about the work of Process Consulting, the following 12 chapters examine each of the Twelve Core Competencies. Each chapter includes two case studies from a wide and diverse group of practicing consultants where the respective competency was clearly in play. In the spirit of Process Consulting, the case studies do not tell you how to do something. Rather, they each tell you a story where the competency was useful, breaking the story down into its basic components. The case studies then invite professional reflection that can be strengthened further through dialogue with others.

As you work through the book, here are several definitions to keep in mind.

Figure 2

Adaptive Moves—These are action steps taken to adapt to change. Typically this change is not fully understood and is revealing itself at the same time that a process is being designed and followed. This grows from the distinction between technical change and adaptive change. Technical moves address known problems with known solutions, while adaptive moves work to discover and innovate in the face of unknown problems with unknown solutions.

Client—This is the organization that retains the Process Consultant, and the word also describes the people of that organization. "Client" is intentionally capitalized throughout the book to signify this layered identity, as in more transactional thinking the term "client" can conjure up the image of a faceless entity holding the checkbook, rather than a diverse group of humans powering an organization. This intersection of people and their organization is where the Process Consultant is found listening, helping, and learning.

Consultant—This is a general term that can mean almost anyone who thinks they have something to offer by selling one's time or intellectual property.

INTRODUCTION

From a Client perspective "consultant" might mean anyone other than an employee retained for a specific task or for access to intellectual property.

Consulting Agreement—Rather than offering a services contract, the Process Consultant establishes Client-defined and Client-owned objectives with the Client, specifically identifying *why, who, what, when, where,* and *how* (see the opening chapter for more about this). This Agreement becomes the statement of work and already begins to form a Process Design with the Client.

Helping—Coming shoulder to shoulder alongside a Client to facilitate a Process Design and any resulting steps that address Client-defined objectives and agenda.

It—Clients often open initial conversations with statements such as *We can't figure it out!* or *It isn't working!* An important part of Process Consulting is to get a clear, Client-defined description of what the word "it" refers to. Client-defined and Client-owned objectives begin with a clear rendering of "it."

Learning—Process Consulting leverages the Client's intention to keep growing and fosters an ongoing process of engagement with the world in combination with self-reflection. Client work is conducted in such a way that action and reflection are part of the process for both the Client and the Process Consultant. Learning then emerges for the benefit of the larger world.

Listening—In our context, this is treated as the high art of bringing one's full self to sincere, attentive, and sustained curiosity where the Client is concerned.

Process Consultant—Someone experienced in being a thought partner alongside a Client. They ask iterative design questions and develop a sequence of steps with a Client to address their objectives. Process Consultants can be recognized by their listening posture, their helping partnership, and their ongoing learning with the Client as the expression of Client service.

Process Design—This is when the Process Consultant collaborates with the Client to design a sequence of steps that a Client pursues to address their stated objectives. The design work is primarily accomplished through robust answers to the iterating questions *why, who, what, when, where,* and *how.*

Understanding the terms above is highly beneficial for Process Consultants who aspire to the Core Competencies detailed in the following chapters.

An Opening Chapter

WWWWWH

Process Consulting began for me in the 1980s. Can it really have been that long ago? I was deeply involved in community work and parish life, and quickly learning that I did not have a firm grasp on fostering groups through the decision-making process.

Working on a master's thesis at the time, I decided to focus on group decision-making, deeply dissatisfied with the methods available to me. Most businesses and non-profits were using the Great Man theory of leadership and decision-making at the time: a person at the top of an organization, by virtue of holding the office, makes decisions carried out by those below him. Associational systems such as professional organizations, political parties, civic organizations, religious denominations, and service clubs, however, tended to use parliamentary procedure à la Robert's Rules of Order. The Great Man might have been efficient but was often not thorough. The parliamentarian way too easily became mind-numbingly thorough and a terrible waste of time and money. Both methods squandered talent. What methods might blend efficiency and thoroughness to create more success for everyone?

This is where discernment methods come into play. At the time most of the work around discernment could be found among the Jesuits and the Friends (Quakers). Very little was written down and most of what was had not been put to the test of social science. Research from the Harvard Negotiation Project was just beginning to be published at that time. That work rounded out the social science literature I used to complete my master's thesis in which I developed a discernment methodology beginning with the iterative questions of *why, who, what, when, where,* and *how.*

An iterative process is simply expressed by these questions, and yet it requires significant mental discipline to make sure all of them are consistently and clearly answered in a sequence. A Process Consultant's Agreement with a Client grows out of completing this iteration so successfully that the satisfied Client recommends the Process Consultant to someone else without being asked to do so (a full measure of achievement).

Kim Stezala and I wrote a white paper[3] a decade ago that still receives wide use. We wrote:

> "Strategic planning methods and tools are so numerous and contradictory that leaders have good reason to trust their own judgment, even if their judgment is flawed and uninformed. Actually, many strategic planning methods come from executives who followed their own judgment and found success. Their success convinced them that what they did in one setting would be successful elsewhere. They launched a consulting practice and then tried to sell their personality and method as an incredible method you can purchase from them. Maybe you've heard the offers, 'Act now and you can get a discount! Purchase level two, the expert level! Become a protégé who can carry the secrets of strategic planning to other companies where you can drop the name of your business guru as your personal friend and give her or him 50% or more of your fees! Then you too can claim to be an international speaker who has consulted with Fortune 500 companies!' Yikes!
>
> "The result? Another product on the market that adds to the confusion, driving even more executives to do it on their own. Those who find success will erroneously believe that they have discovered the magical organizational elixir that works wherever it is drunk—just follow the

directions and 'do it like they done it' even though the situation is entirely different! Furthermore, most strategic planning products do not have a solution for situations in which previous planning efforts were begun and then scrapped, implemented and then only partially successful, or adapted on the fly because of changing circumstances. Business-celebrity driven products and methods usually have no mechanism to diagnose and fix work that is already underway.

"What self-proclaimed experts repeatedly fail to understand is that it was the **process** that made their strategy successful:

> **Armed with the right reasons,**
>
> **the right people figured it out**
>
> **with the right insight**
>
> **at the right place**
>
> **at the right time**
>
> **with the right approach**

"Remove any one of these factors from the recipe and even the most sophisticated or exciting method struggles to find success. If each element is present, even the most rudimentary method can take an organization forward."

Right Reasons form the *why*, the mission of the Agreement. *Why* comes first, before anything else.

Right People, the *who*, demonstrates:
- Who decides,

- Who does the work,
- Who supervises,
- Who needs to be consulted,
- Who funds the work,
- And who manages communication up and downstream.
- All of those identified in the *who* section need to agree, explicitly and definitionally, on the *why*.

Right Insight, the *what*, is the list of criteria for a successful process. Developing a mutually acknowledged criteria for success can be complicated because the criteria come from individual and subjective points of view. Depending on one's personality, criteria may be based on thoughts (perhaps expressed negatively as fear), intuition (perhaps expressed negatively in anger), or emotion (perhaps expressed negatively as guilt or shame). The way through the complexity is not by ensuring everyone agrees but rather that everyone's point of view is acknowledged, understood, and included in the list in some way.

Right Place, the *where*, is sometimes not needed, but, if any specific geography is included, it should be specifically identified. (Note: sometimes "geography" is someone or something's domain in which the work will take place—not just a specific geography.)

Right Time, the *when*, identifies deadlines and specific time markers along the way. It is good to set them, even artificially.

Right Approach, the *how*, details specific action steps to accomplish the *what*, and by *when*.

A Process Consulting Agreement articulates WWWWWH details. The words *why, who, what, when, where*, and *how* are built right into a Process Consulting Agreement. They are markers demonstrating a process orientation, a Client-centeredness, and a commitment to Client collaboration. Even if these words are not explicit in the Client Consulting Agreement, they need to be easily identifiable. Without this clarity and explicitness, Process Consultants and people connected to the Client quickly find themselves working toward different goals.

The iterative process of identifying WWWWWH enables the Process Consultant to assume a listening posture from the beginning. The iteration provides the opportunity to reflect back to the Client what the Process Consultant hears and understands before they begin assisting with anything. How embarrassing it would be to start in with a Client only to discover you are talking about a subject other than what the Client intended!

Some Clients will think out loud, using early conversations with the Process Consultant as a foil to begin figuring out what they want. What they say the first time or two may not ultimately remain in the final Agreement. WWWWWH help Client find clarity and focus for actions that follow.

Here is a fun way we can illustrate the work of coaxing out those stubborn elements of a process (Fig. 3):

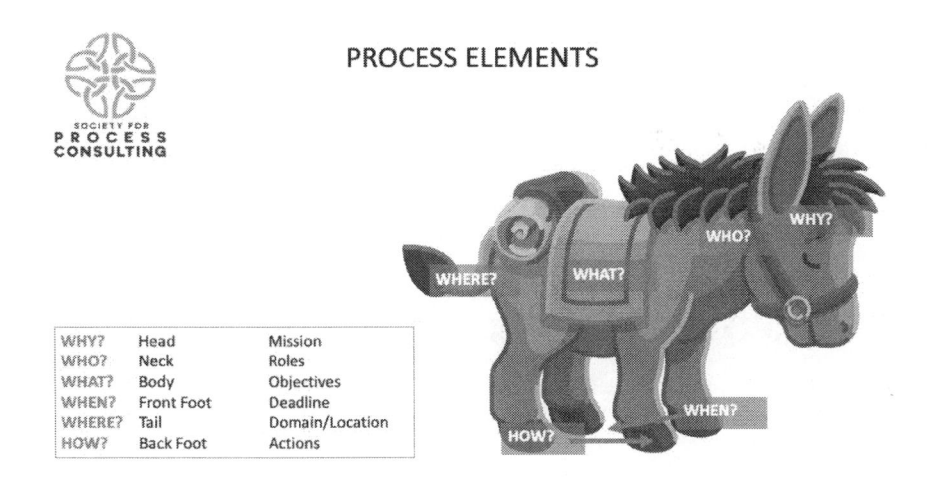

PROCESS ELEMENTS

WHY?	Head	Mission
WHO?	Neck	Roles
WHAT?	Body	Objectives
WHEN?	Front Foot	Deadline
WHERE?	Tail	Domain/Location
HOW?	Back Foot	Actions

Figure 3

Why, the mission, is the "brain" of the process. It is the mission of the Agreement. The Process Consultant and the key Client representatives need to be in explicit agreement about this mission. The explicit "yes" to this mission builds the ownership needed to follow through and execute a process successfully.

Who, the people who play important roles, are the neck that turns the entire process beast in the intended direction. Each role must be identified! Some people or entities will play multiple roles, especially in smaller or newer organizations or with projects of limited scope or duration. Even so, clarifying roles before a process begins prevents many a problem as the project is completed.

What, the body, is the substance of the process, the criteria for success, the objectives you aim to meet. You don't need total agreement from everyone involved on the inclusion or prioritization of the criteria, but they need to see that what they care about is included on the list. They also need to demonstrate that they recognize and understand what others care about as a sign of success.

When, the front foot, represents the deadline. We work backwards from there to *how*. If there is no fixed deadline, you will need to set one. A deadline helps you to work backwards to create a sequence of actions and determine how much time there is to complete them.

Where, the domain or geography of the process, is the tail. Sometimes it is crucial and sometimes it is not.

How, the back foot, is the sequence of actions that walk us through the process from beginning to end. This list will often read very much like the key dates identified in *when*. The difference is that *when* identifies a timetable whereas the *how* demonstrates the sequence of actions. Being deliberate about answering both helps a scope and sequence to emerge.

EVER SINCE THEN...

Process Consulting as identified in this book draws on these discernment roots and iterative questions. Over the 35 years since I wrote that thesis, the field has come into its own, and its contributors have built a veritable ecosystem of resources. Ed Schein has provided a wealth of works on process

AN OPENING CHAPTER: WWWWWH

consultation. Peter Block has created resources on developing an integrity-laden consulting practice, with Etienne Wengerd chiming in on the shape and function of Communities of Practice. E.F. Schumacher's contributions on meaning-making in one's economic life are also invaluable. All these great thinkers and doers have come together to expand the available resources for Process Consultants who care about the impact of our work as we develop people and organizations—jointly transforming for a more vibrant future.

The tap root for all this remains our ability to acquire and retain clarity about *why*, *who*, *what*, *when*, *where*, and *how*. The Twelve Core Competencies help Process Consultants and organizational leaders reduce the world's complexities to these simpler lines of sight necessary to move forward with faith in our ability to accomplish something meaningful together.

LISTENING

The First Core Competency

LISTENING ACTIVELY AND COMPREHENSIVELY

Jack Hartman made a children's music video[4] about whole body listening that every ants-in-their-pants child must love. The silly dancing and sugar-coated music in the video makes an important point. To learn we must get our eyes, ears, hands, feet, bodies, brains, and hearts open, focused, and ready to learn. Without focusing all our antennae, without being fully present, we will not fully absorb, understand, or retain what we are trying to learn.

Where is your *head* as you start reading this book? Is it here? In the present moment? Free from distractions?

Where is your *heart*? Are your emotions settled and placed properly so you can attend, without fear, anger, or anxiety?

And where is your *body*? Is it at rest, able to attend to the content that follows? Is it opened?

Are you breathing?

Are you able to fully concentrate? This is what active and whole-body listening is. **Full. Concentration.**

Active listening is the posture of the Process Consultant. Posture involves the whole self: head, heart, soul, and body. The active posture of a Process Consultant requires:

- A head that is in the present moment with the Client.
- A heart that is full of love for the person(s) and the organization—who the Client and organization were, are, and will become.
- A soulful, appreciative awareness that the conversation with the Client is deeply layered in context and meaning.
- A body that is tuned and attuned to the source(s) of information.

Those committed to using their whole self to listen know that thinking or emoting comes after the listening, not during. It takes full concentration to empty oneself from distractions, to square one's body to the source of information, and to hold a focused and attentive gaze while offering trust and safety to people who are facing a problem or an opportunity that they find challenging.

These are the elements of active and whole-body listening:

Eyes—Our eyes are on the sources of information. Our eyes move away from the speaker when we start thinking about what we are hearing rather than absorbing the experience of listening. Our eyes are a tell that we aren't fully listening anymore. *Observe this in yourself in conversations to come.*

Ears—Additional sounds or movement distract from our capacity to hear specific word choices and what they mean to the speaker. Our brain must divide into subtasks to try to catch up, as well as to fill in gaps about context with our guesses. Deep comprehension becomes minimal. *Take note of how frequently you find yourself tempted to pretend you fully listened.*

Mouth—Mostly this means our mouths are closed, letting natural impressions, thoughts and reactions pass by because we have not heard

LISTENING ACTIVELY AND COMPREHENSIVELY

everything yet. If they are important, they will return to us. *Remember the acronyms* WAIT[5] *and* WAIST[6] *as you enter important conversations.*

Hands—Our hands lead us in supporting or destabilizing our listening posture. Our hands enhance or harm spatial boundaries. *Pay attention to where you place your hands when you are in conversation with someone.*

Feet—Our feet point our bodies toward where we really want to be. Feet also take us nearer to or further from sources of information. They can help us show our interest and create an environment to take in the information; conversely, they can reveal that we don't really want to be there. Pay attention to the feet of your conversation partner(s), as well! Do they really want to be here speaking with you? *Take notice of where you and they want to be as a conversation begins.*

Shoulders—Our shoulders need to face the source of information—especially when that source is speaking. This points all our sensual antennae to the source of information. It takes active concentration and practice to make this our normal listening posture. *Ask yourself if you are turned even slightly turned away.*

Brain—Comprehension, and its lack, both settle in the brain. The brain is where input from all the senses is organized so it can be restated using all the elements of active listening. This is the tool to engage curiosity and ask questions to help clarify what we think we know, and to demonstrate that we have listened and comprehended before we offer insight, analysis, or recommendations. Take time to reflect after a conversation. *Was your brain on the same frequency as you listened, or was it on a parallel frequency because you were thinking while others were speaking?*

Heart—Our heart rate reflects our serenity as well as our anxiety. It is affected by our care for our bodies and the rhythm and depth of our breathing. Calm helps us attune to where, when, and with whom we are, to turn outward to another and offer sincere empathy. It allows us to be our authentic self, bringing love to the person(s), the context, and the situation we intend to address. *Pause to notice how your heart rate reflects your agitation or calm during a conversation.*

The Process Consultant cannot be elsewhere than the room (virtual or real) that they are in, with the people and organization they are with, in any other body than their own, and not in any other moment than the now. Active listening grows from this understanding.

Active listening is a singular aid to comprehensive listening; however, it is no guarantee of comprehension.

Comprehension needs to be, well, comprehensive. You'll know you've got "it" when the Client says, *Yes! You said it better than I did.*

The "it" in that previous sentence is what both the Process Consultant and the Client are after. The Client must express the "it" first, before anyone—Client or Process Consultant—can claim comprehension. The Client is talking with the Process Consultant about this thing, this adaptive and complex scenario, that they might barely understand.[7] They don't know exactly what "it" is or how to address it. They don't fully comprehend it themselves. How can the Process Consultant claim to fully understand something the Client doesn't yet understand? And why would they be talking with you if they did? Maybe the Process Consultant has seen something similar, but if it is an adaptive and complex change in a specific context, then their "it" is unique.

The Client is trying to comprehend the problem that they need help to describe. The Process Consultant asks the iterative questions of *why*, who, *what*, *when*, *where*, and *how*, to make comprehension comprehensive—to help draw out and organize details. Iterative questions bring a comprehensiveness to comprehension for both Clients and Process Consultants.

Further questions can be asked within *why*, *who*, *what*, *when*, *where*, and *how* in order deepen comprehension. One of the most powerful questions in the Process Consultant's toolbox is, *Is there anything else?*[8]

The iterative questions build mutual comprehension of what is known and understood—and what isn't. These questions help to design a mutually agreed upon set of action steps toward agreed upon ends. The Process Consultant uses the information gained by asking these questions to reflect back an organized expression of what they are hearing. This gives the Client an opportunity to respond in one of two ways:

> *Yes! You said it better than I did.*
> *That's not it exactly. What I meant was* . . . (which sends the Process Consultant back into active listening mode to clarify further).

Iterative questions help the Process Consultant strike and hold an active listening posture from the first interaction with the Client.

By necessity, the Process Consultant's comprehension is going to be different than the Client's.

The Client is trying to understand and address their "it." The Process Consultant is providing an active listening presence to describe "it" in the fullest measure, often by:

- Identifying the issue(s) underlying the presenting issue (the Client's "it") so that "it" can be addressed successfully.
- Helping the Client's subjective expression of the "it" become an external objective, so that a whole system—both people and processes—participate together with a commonly held understanding.
- Bringing a framework to help guide the Client's perception and thinking. Other words or phrases like lens, *experiment, correlation, similarity, intuitive leap, or preferred future* are ways to help the Client to freshly and more accurately examine their "it," and for both the Client and the Process Consultant to comprehend more comprehensively.

THE FIRST CORE COMPETENCY

The Client needs to comprehend their "it," but they might not yet be actively listening to their context. The Process Consultant needs to bring active and whole-body listening to the Client and the context from the start. This level of active listening for comprehension is both art and science of the Process Consulting craft. Process Consultants listen to what the Client might not be able to hear themselves.

Active and whole-body listening are encouraged in coaching, facilitating, moderating, and presenting, as well as in Process Consulting. Active and comprehensive listening specifically applied to Process Consulting is the means to enshrine a Client's objectives at the heart of a Client Agreement. The Client's intentions become the statement of work rather than the Consultant's prescription for the Client.

CONCLUDING THOUGHT

To bring themselves more readily to this level of listening and comprehension, the Process Consultant must do their own work to be self-aware, to constantly care for their own heart-soul-mind-strength well-being, to be fully present and curious, to not be anxious about whether the Client will sign with them, and to bring empathy and authenticity to the relationship. Active listening toward comprehensive comprehension, then, becomes an attribute of the Process Consultant. It is part of their character. It is their natural posture.

Listening Actively and Comprehensively
CASE STUDIES

1. Is the future as bright as it seems?

Background. Little Valley Arts Cooperative recently moved onto an heirloom farm that somehow remained intact as the city grew up around it. The donating family had lived on the land for six generations, able to trace the deed to a land grant direct from President Benjamin Harrison. The family recently uncovered evidence that their inheritance was possible because of unjust treatment of Native Americans. In making their gift, they wanted assurances that Native American artists and art would become a centerpiece for the Cooperative's mission. After consideration, the board agreed, adjusting the mission, strategy, and board structure of the Little Valley Arts Cooperative.

Made up primarily of painters and sculptors, the Cooperative was excited that the new location also allowed for construction of a first-rate kiln in the barn. A community of eager ceramicists, which would further expand the Cooperative's capacity, was already forming. The future was bright.

Of the family who had agreed to donate the farm to the Little Valley Arts Cooperative, two sisters and a brother were still living. Since this gift would be formalized sometime after the end of the lease in the old warehouse across town, Little Valley Arts Cooperative was allowed to move in before technically receiving the gift of the farm. They would pay a modest rent in the meantime.

Two weeks ago, the brother died without a clear will or estate plan in place. His four children quickly contacted a lawyer and made it known to their aunts that they wanted the farm sold and added to their father's estate to be distributed among them and their children. A key factor in this dispute was extreme medical expenses for a granddaughter with cerebral palsy; these expenses had nearly led to her family's bankruptcy. The proceeds of the farm would be a great help. The family was open to having the Little Valley Arts Cooperative purchase their shares of the land and for their aunts to donate their own portions. They simply wanted their share in cash. If attorneys for all parties could not strike an agreement, a probate hearing was scheduled in two months.

The Board Chair of the Little Valley Arts Cooperative contacted Brenda Armitage, a Process Consultant, asking if she could work with the Board to figure out their options and how to respond. Brenda began working through the iterative questions in her conversation with the Board Chair.

—Mark L. Vincent

FOR PROCESS CONSULTANT DISCUSSION

1. What information can you glean from the above paragraphs using these questions:

- Why is this important?
- Who would play what role in determining options and how to respond?
- What might form a comprehensive set of objectives that benefit all parties? What would the specific objectives be for the Little Valley Arts Cooperative?
- When does the Board of the Little Valley Arts Cooperative want/need to be ready with its response?
- Where are the domains of each party involved, and how are they overlapping?
- How would the Little Valley Arts Cooperative proceed from here?

2. What other questions might Brenda ask that would invite the client to:

LISTENING ACTIVELY AND COMPREHENSIVELY

- More fully understand the background of the issue they face?
- Listen to themselves also?
- Discover what opportunities also appeared while exploring the problem?

2. Complications when operating castles

Background. Devereaux & Hastings, Ltd. is a boutique commercial real estate investment company located in Edinburgh, Scotland, with a few additional offices throughout the United Kingdom. Maurice Deveraux and Hiram Hastings formed the company in the late 1800s as representatives of landowners to maintain and transact their estate holdings. Over nearly 150 years, the company has been passed down to heirs of Maurice and Hiram and is now owned by their great-grandsons, Niles and Hiram IV, who are in their late sixties. Niles is married to Claudette and Hiram IV is married to Grace.

D&H's primary focus is acquiring high-value, historic properties and converting them into other uses, including various types of lodging, restaurants, private schools, company retreats, and research centers. These are castles, manors, homes, buildings, and land holdings of families without a known heir, or whose current owners no longer desire or cannot afford to maintain the property. Upon acquiring a property, D&H designs and oversees the conversion process, then manages the new business, or provides capital to a new owner with or without conversion.

D&H typically convert three to five large properties, and several smaller ones each year, manage around 20 businesses, and capitalize 10 other sales. D&H's current portfolio value under management is around £100M, and it has £250M in capital investment. Niles and Hiram IV also have substantial personal real estate holdings from generations of family purchases, some connected to British nobility.

Over several decades, the owners and their executive leaders have developed an independent, but closely associated, team of realtors, lawyers, bank executives, architects, construction and remodeling contractors, decorators, and property and business managers—made mostly of their children and other family members. Although there have been minor disagreements or misunderstandings over the years, the company has maintained a culture of unity and loyalty among these various business units. They also have maintained a reputation among their peers and Clients of integrity, efficiency, and discretion.

Niles and Hiram IV have been in the process of grooming their children to move into leadership and eventual ownership of the company. Niles has two daughters: Celeste is married to Adam, an American who inherited a private investment firm from his father, Great Lakes Capital (GLC), with offices in Chicago, Singapore, and Zagreb; and Sade, who is adopted from Kenya, is married to Tobias, a Kenyan businessman. Hiram IV has a son, Hiram V, who is married to Anna.

After consulting with the leadership of both GLC and D&H, Adam retained the writers of this case study as Process Consultants for the two companies.

PROCESS DESIGN

Why are we doing this? There are three intertwined issues where D&H/GLC asked for perspective and guidance:

- Over the last two years the operating landscape for both companies has been substantially affected by Brexit and the COVID pandemic.

- When Adam and Celeste married, Niles and Hiram IV suggested a merger between D&H and GLC to create a new international firm.

LISTENING ACTIVELY AND COMPREHENSIVELY

- In addition, Niles and Hiram IV are ready to retire and transfer D&H to their children.

These are each complex issues that have multiple decision points. Niles and Hiram IV desire to clarify the emotional, relational, and operational realities that will affect the new company and their transition into retirement. They also want an objective outside party to facilitate the discussions and decision-making process for each area.

In the initial contract negotiation, we described our approach to consulting as a process of inquiry and guidance—a co-discovery of solutions of what might work best.

Who **are we going to listen to?** All the stakeholders have personal, professional, financial, and emotional investments in the issues. Our desire was to hear the perspective and concerns of all the key decision makers in a way that felt safe and non-threatening to them. We knew it would be time-consuming, but necessary to meet with individuals separately first: Adam, Niles, Hiram IV, and their wives. Then each of the D&H children and their spouses, and with the six executive directors of each geographic area in each company.

Eighteen personal conversations told us what each of them felt about the company and the other leaders, and what they thought about the issues, considering their own expectations and needs. We were able to hear the passions, commitment, concerns, and fears of each person, and form a picture of the culture, strengths, and vulnerabilities of each company.

As our consulting process continues, we will meet with the owners together, the senior leadership teams, and those who will be supporting them in each transition.

What **have the stakeholders told us so far that will allow us to help them?**

- We are passionate about our company, we are grateful for each other and our employees, and we want to see our new business be even more successful.

- Our spouses are grateful they have been brought into the discussions, and they are generally supportive of our direction, as long as we all keep listening to each other.
- D&H

    —We love our family—immediate and extended across our company—and we want to see them continue to prosper for several more generations.
    —We're not perfect, and we have our scraps here and there, but keeping a relationship is more important that keeping a couple quid.
    —We want to see these transitions, the merger and the retirements, happen with the same commitment to unity and mutual respect we have always maintained.
    —We're not sure what it will be like becoming an international company, but we're committed to making it work, and we're excited to serve a much larger group of Clients.

- GLC

    —We are excited about merging with such a highly respected British company, D&H.
    —We're not sure how the new leadership structure will work, but we'll create something that takes care of our employees and our Clients.
    —It's been so hard to keep a good attitude in the last year.
    —We need to make this transition as stress free as possible, and something that brings energy and hope.

- We have hard work ahead to run our new company well

    —We need to maintain business operations with new local and global challenges.
    —We must maintain a healthy culture—physically, emotionally, relationally.

LISTENING ACTIVELY AND COMPREHENSIVELY

　　—Brexit brings legal and financial changes for business, property and land ownership.
　　—The COVID-19 pandemic has been the impetus behind more effective virtual meetings, management, and decisions as well as personal losses, and restrictions/closings that affect all our operations and travel.

- Merger

　　—D&H and GLC are committed to working together well; we need to solidify our trust base and match expectations.
　　How are we going to ensure all our leaders are in the right roles?
　　—How do we develop a new mission and purpose for our new company?
　　—What does our new organizational structure look like?

- Niles & Hiram IV retirement

　　—We trust Celeste, Sade, and Hiram V as the new owners of D&H.
　　—We think Tobias would be a good director of operations.
　　—We are excited about the merger with GLC, and for Adam to join our ownership team.
　　—We need to negotiate a fair ownership transfer.
　　—We need to move our real estate holdings into the new company.

When do the companies want to proceed to the next step?

- The need to address the effects of Brexit and the pandemic is immediate and ongoing, so getting to a set of actions and timeline may be a priority.

- The merger is in the early stages of discussion; our role will be to use the perspective and expectations from the stakeholders, discover any possible roadblocks, and help them formulate a plan, in addition to the financial and legal input they will need.

THE FIRST CORE COMPETENCY

- The basic succession plan for the owners has been in place for several years, so we will discover with them if there are any relationship or leadership issues to work through, any additional input they might need, and an appropriate timeline.

Where **will these conversations take place?**
Due to the restrictions on travel, we held our first discussions virtually. Subsequently, we met in person with Adam and some of his leaders in his Chicago boardroom. We will continue to monitor the global travel situation and decide together about meeting locations, whether in-person or virtual.

How **will we continue to listen and help these companies?**
- We completed the initial stage of listening and learning from each stakeholder, so we can help them discover what they need for each area.
- With that background and perspective, we will group gatherings to hear the corporate voice:
- Adam, Niles, and Hiram IV

    –GLC leadership team
    –D&H leadership team

- We will help the owners and their leadership teams develop strategies for their current challenges:

    –Continued remote planning/negotiations/management meetings
    Effects of Brexit legal and financial changes in UK and Europe
    Supply chain issues for conversion and remodeling projects
    –Employment challenges for investment account executives, construction projects, property management

- We will facilitate meetings where the foundations of the newly merged company are formed.

    –Mission/Purpose/Values Statement
    –Organizational and Leadership Structure

LISTENING ACTIVELY AND COMPREHENSIVELY

- We will facilitate meetings to create the succession strategy for Niles and Hiram IV.

  —JOHN ERICKSON AND DENNIS HUMPHREY

FOR PROCESS CONSULTANT DISCUSSION

1. So far, the children of Niles and Hiram IV have expressed no major concerns about their relationship together and with Adam, or their mutual ownership of D&H. Do you think there is more to be discovered here? What else might be asked to discover not only what needs to be done but also what they are willing to do?
2. Do you notice any dynamics the Process Consultants are not capturing? How would you draw attention to them?
3. How might the Process Consultants have to adjust their listening style when moving between in-person and virtual meetings?
4. Does anything in this Process Design seem to be missing? Does the how point back to address the why?
5. How would you facilitate the discussion with the Devereauxs and the Hastings around the retirement and succession of Niles and Hiram IV? Who else would you suggest attend that meeting? How would you guide their process of defining the outcomes? How would you handle unmet expectations or disagreements? How would you foster their willingness and ability to listen to each other?

The Second Core Competency

LISTENING CONCEPTUALLY AND CONTEXTUALLY

A person intent on developing their listening capacity quickly learns they are never done. With every layer of intensive listening, we uncover a deeper layer still. As an illustration, the Core Competency of Listening Actively and Comprehensively (see the previous chapter) advocates that we are completely present so as not to miss information. The Process Consultant is actively listening to comprehensively comprehend. Deciding to listen conceptually and contextually moves active listening deeper still.

A Process Consultant should understand that listening conceptually and contextually may bring their comprehension beyond what the Client currently perceives. Their creation of a safe environment in which the Client can keep working out their *why, who, what, when, where,* and *how* helps the Client begin to listen also; and in this listening, to begin to perceive possibilities beyond their current comprehension. This level of comprehension may open doors to discovery or insight for both the Client and the Process Consultant. *Discovery and insight make adaptive moves possible.*

THE SECOND CORE COMPETENCY

The competent Process Consultant listens so well that the Client also starts listening to themselves. Together, the Client and Process Consultant explore new territory. Together, they discover that there is something possible beyond what can currently be measured and perceived about the Client's desired goals. Together, they begin to discern how to move from where the Client is toward where the Client intends to be.

A sign the Process Consultant has listened well is when they have nothing to say for a moment after the Client finishes speaking. They don't need to express themselves. The Process Consultant is still absorbing— "aware-ing." The Process Consultant's thinking and responding takes a back seat to this level of listening. It is good for the Process Consultant to breathe in such a moment and trust that their brain did not abandon them. It is in the slowing down and aware-ing that insight can grow. Questions and responses will follow in their time.

The Core Competency of Listening for the Process Consultant, then, is not just listening *to* the Client. It is listening *for and with* the Client.

The ECHO Listening Assessment helps a person consider how they might build their listening skill. By drawing on the overview[9] provided with the assessment, we can learn more about listening *to* and *for* and *with*.

Listening *to* the Client primarily involves forming trusting relationships as well as an accurate and comprehensive organization of what the Client is saying. This ties to the first Core Competency of Listening Actively and Comprehensively. Listening at this level answers *why* and *who* questions and begins to identify answers to *what*.

Listening *for* and *with* the Client involves conceptual and analytical skills. These skills tie to the second Core Competency of Listening Conceptually and Contextually, our subject in this chapter. Listening at this level sets the stage for Process Design (Listening), specific Process Consultation (Helping), and implementation/evaluation (Learning). This set of skills helps to identify responses to *what, when, where,* and *how*.

Listening actively, comprehensively, conceptually, and contextually are habits we continue developing all our lives. No one will be perfect at listening.

LISTENING CONCEPTUALLY AND CONTEXTUALLY

The competent Process Consultant knows this and continues to grow their listening capacity.

To listen CONCEPTUALLY, we listen along with the Client to their word choices and then for what they mean. This is especially important in the *why* and *what* portions of setting up a Consulting Agreement—the Client's internal agreement and agreement with the Process Consultant about what will be addressed and how. The Process Consultant and the Client need the same operating definitions or else the listening hasn't happened, helping cannot be effective, and learning will be limited. Further, the Client's team who will work on this Agreement needs to agree on definitions, or else it will severely impede any Process Design, implementation, and evaluation. Finally, all those in the orbit of the final Client Agreement need to understand it, even if they do not completely agree. Who can participate meaningfully if they do not first comprehend?

Consider the often used and practical conceptual words and phrases such as *mission, membership, profit, fiscal year end, customer, job description, hiring practice, consultant, finance,* and *termination.* Can you assume you and the Client mean the same thing? Really?

What words or phrases would you add to the above list? When a Client uses a conceptual word or phrase in a manner that may mean something different to various participants in the process, how do you proceed to ensure you are all in agreement on the definition? How do you do this during the first steps of a consulting engagement?

Once underway, do you follow a rhythm of reinforcing conceptual agreement? A best practice to ensure starting and ongoing conceptual agreement is to begin all Client facilitation using the following sequence:

1. Here is why we are working together—a reminder of the mission of the Client Agreement.[10]
2. That is where we were.
3. Here is where we are (Do we need to make any adjustments?).
4. This, then, is what we are doing now.
5. There is where we go next.

To listen contextually, we listen with the Client for insight into any complications or concerns underneath the presenting issue. We might call this *listening underneath*. Insight starts with what is observable and can be described, measured, and analyzed, then repeatedly asking *What else?* until the Client has nothing more to add. Listening underneath gathers and organizes information, then asks *Why?* the proverbial five times, digging down to bedrock underneath.

Sometimes the Client is out of touch with their context. A useful tool can be a SWOT analysis[11], identifying a Client's Strengths, Weaknesses, Opportunities, and Threats, especially when this SWOT pairs with a broader environmental scan.[12] This level of analysis provides a contextual framework for everyone's common reference. It helps the Client listen underneath and alongside the Process Consultant. Contextual understanding at this level gathers tinder to ignite potential insight.

Listening contextually also helps the Process Consultant and Client listen for implications should the Client continue or not continue their course. This is *listening forward*.

If we are considering implications, we are determining what can be predicted based on current trends or if a new variable is introduced. Listening forward asks *What if?* The Process Consultant and Client are reaching out to sense how deep the pain runs and/or how significant opportunities could be.

Some Clients struggle to conceive of implications. Perhaps they are quite strong operationally. This strength can be a hindrance to imagining what could be because the organization's focus is on managing what it already has. A useful tool here is an exercise of Futures Thinking[13], a specialized form of multi-scenario planning[14], bringing future implications to the present, immersing the Client in those implications, and creating safe and patient settings for considering what might be done.

Listening contextually is also *listening across*. This type of listening notices current and/or past scenarios that relate to the current scenario the Client describes. Past scenarios are not necessarily correlations and are rarely, if ever, a sole cause. They are best thought of as resonances or echoes of places and scenes the Client and Process Consultant might draw upon to see if any principles or applications might be borrowed, adopted, or adapted to the current context.

Intersections noticed by listening across are often convergent dynamics coming together. Listening across asks *Where else?* and *Have we seen this before?* Listening across reaches across time and space to pull multi-disciplinary and multi-scenario possibilities into the conversation, making the contextual understanding even more comprehensive. This is a particularly useful question when working with adaptive change.

Triangulation[15] is one tool that shines light on intersections and confirm their reality to a specific context. This is not the toxic form of triangulation where stress between two people is communicated indirectly to and through a third person. In this context, triangulation is a form of navigating with many applications: in this case a way to pinpoint where the uncertain Client is, as well as where they may choose to go. By looking at an issue from at least three different perspectives and identifying commonalities, the Client gains assurance that anything felt intuitively, or any conclusion drawn from one data point, is either well-founded or of diminished concern.[16]

Listening contextually is also *listening beyond.* This is intuitive listening, listening for the Client's readiness to move above and beyond what is known and with a focus on the future. It hearkens back to Aristotle's three forms of knowledge, especially *phronesis*, the third of these:

   a. *Episteme*—intellectual knowledge of concepts and causes.
   b. *Techne*—knowledge that enables us to perform tasks with a practiced confidence.
   c. *Phronesis*—an ability to bring together knowledge and values in making wise judgement in new and previously unexperienced circumstances.

Listening beyond allows for awareness of intuitive leaps that might be made, often felt in the body before they can be articulated or are articulated as a completed state before details are developed. Listening beyond is a jump

THE SECOND CORE COMPETENCY

to a potential experiment or solution statement. We ask questions like *Why not?* or *Could we?*

Many organizations struggle with intuitive leaps. Perhaps they had an entrepreneurial founder whose skill at sniffing out what was next has yet to be replaced following their departure. Perhaps the organization is so data-driven that their analytic skills leave them paralyzed to act.

The gut-check[17] is a physical process a person and an organization can convert to guardrails that foster and guide intuition. Yes, even a gut-check can be a process-oriented tool! The Process Consultant and Client can literally close their eyes and ask themselves what their bodies are telling them in a moment where outcomes are hard to predict. They can also use the Client's mission statement as a sort of North Star to help them stay oriented and navigate forward when they are considering territory beyond where they are now, and where there is no reliable data.

Contextual listening is listening underneath (*What else? Why?*), forward (*What if?*), across (*Where else?*) and beyond (*Why not? Could we?*). Listening at this level does not just happen in conversation. It means digging into Client artifacts in preparation for a Client engagement. Triangulation comes into play here also as the Process Consultant schools themselves on the Client from several related angles. Mutual gathering and reviewing a relevant set of meeting minutes, strategic plans, budgets with current financials, staff reports, charter documents, positional statements, Client-produced white papers, and/or performance metrics—especially leading indicators—are a means for the Process Consultant and the Client to begin this level of listening.

The Process Consultant is wise to understand how contextual listening inspires and activates the Client now and into the future. Consider two examples.

Example One: The ancient King Solomon is said to have been confronted with the dilemma of two female sex workers who shared a home, and each had a baby. One of the babies died during the night and in the darkness the bereaved mother switched the children. In the light of morning, the other mother readily noticed the switch and demanded her child back. Which woman was to be believed? King Solomon called for a sword to divide the surviving baby, at which point the real mother offered to give up her claim on the child so that it might live, while the grieving mother was willing to lose both children. King Solomon returned the baby to the real mother as he recognized her sacrificial love for the child.

King Solomon could not know for certain that this would be the outcome. Looking back on the story we can see how astute use of contextual listening provided some guidance. He:

- *Listened underneath*—The presenting issue was the dispute over the child. The underlying issue was the lives of these mothers and their children—people treating others as if they were things, pieces of property, rather than as human beings who possess dignity and a right to flourish.

- *Listened forward*—Solomon was aware of implications growing from the dispute. This was not just a matter of discerning which mother was the one who lost her child. The surviving child's welfare and childhood was also at stake.

- *Listened across*—Disputes over parentage, adultery, incestuous rape, murder, betrayal, and intrigue provided the backdrop during Solomon's own childhood in a polygamous household. This was far from unfamiliar territory to him. The two women in front of him could just as easily have been his own mother and one of the other wives of his father.

- *Listened beyond*—Thinking underneath, forward and across provides a form of triangulation that can result in the intuitive insight Solomon achieves here. The real mother would not further jeopardize the life of the child. So, Solomon calls for a sword to change the terms of the debate. No longer is it a dispute over who is the mother. He changes the terms to the child's welfare. New data emerges and a wiser decision is made.

Example Two: Maya Angelou's recitation of her poem *We Hear You* at the 100th anniversary of the Urban League[18] provides a powerful illustration of contextual listening—of listening deeply and then reflecting back. It is not just the words she wrote; it is in her artful recitation to a community whose lived experience has been captured. The choice of words shows she has listened conceptually and contextually. The audience is aligned with her, but not because she is saying something new and interesting. Rather, she articulates what they feel in their hearts and live in their bodies. A standing ovation erupts.

The Process Consultant can ask themselves these evaluative questions about listening conceptually and contextually:

- Does my pledge to listen to the Client extend to this level of heart openness, full attention, and complete awareness of the Client?

- Can I wait until I have listened at the soul level: actively, comprehensively, conceptually, contextually before I speak and show I have listened? And, before I offer any expertise?

CONCLUDING THOUGHT

While listening full-dimensionally is important, no-one does it perfectly or so profoundly, wisely, or artfully as the above examples display. Certainly, no one can always do so. And it is good to also recognize that no Client can fully describe everything related to the issues they want to address, especially the first time they articulate their "it." This is why the Community of Practice[19] surrounding a Process Consultant is helpful. Such a community provides colleagues who can complement the Process Consultant's own skill. This is why a partnership with the Client to Listen, Help and Learn together is so much more effective. Even further, this is why an iterative and generative approach over time has the better opportunity to help Clients make their adaptive moves. Over time and with patient effort we together make up for our individual flaws.

Listening Conceptually and Contextually

CASE STUDIES

1. Enrollment pressures

Background. Windy River Head Start is an early childhood education program for children ages 0-5 serving children and families in a local tribal community. The program is working on a plan to achieve and maintain full enrollment.

The program is funded to serve 30 children ages 0-2 including expectant mothers and 68 children 3-5 years old. Current enrollment is 20 children ages 0-2 and 50 children ages 3-5. The local school district provides a state funded Pre-K option for children 4 years old. There is also a charter elementary school in the community run by the tribe as well as a tribally-funded childcare program. All tribal programs in the community are immersed in their native language and culture. The community is geographically remote with the nearest town 45 minutes away. The tribe has a healthy, although limited, economic base providing employment opportunities for about 35% of its community members.

Windy River Head Start has struggled with achieving full enrollment for the last two program years. Program administrators are engaging in strategic planning; however, they are unsure of which data sources and stakeholders to include. The program is feeling pressure to meet full enrollment requirements to maintain their current funding level, and they have requested technical assistance to assist with strategic planning and in developing a plan for full enrollment.

PROCESS DESIGN

Why **is this being worked at?** Windy River Head Start must meet their specific funded levels of enrollment per federal guidelines or risk a reduction of the grant funds they were awarded. The program has not been able to maintain a waitlist of eligible children for the past three years and has been under-enrolled in each age group for the past two years. Community assessment data needs to be analyzed for population trends, birth rates, other early childhood education providers, etc. to determine community needs and viable program options. Options include exploring whether a reduction in enrollment is warranted and how to maintain current funding with quality improvement measures.

Who **is involved and what are they doing?**
- The Windy River Head Start director and the Tribal Council, as the grant recipient, are the final decision-makers.

- The assigned Head Start Training and Technical Assistance Specialist (TTA Specialist) will facilitate a strategic planning session with program administrators to determine data sources and stakeholders needed, review the community assessment process, and provide on-going assistance with data evaluation and programming planning related to achieving and maintaining full enrollment.

- The Windy River Head Start staff will conduct the community assessment, gather and analyze data, consult with stakeholders, etc. as determined by the program Director.

- The assigned Office of Head Start (OHS) Program Specialist for Windy River Head Start will be included in discussions and kept in the communication loop because any program option changes will need OHS approval before being implemented.

- The Windy River Head Start Tribal and Policy Council (as the governing board entities) will also review and approve all final plans.
- The Windy River Head Start director is the main point of contact and will ensure communication loops are in place and followed.

***What* criteria for success will be used?**
- Achieves full funded enrollment by the end of the current program year.
- Maintains full enrollment once achieved as well as a healthy waitlist.
- Develops an enrollment plan that:

    –Features program option changes if needed.

    –Details sustainable enrollment by age groups.

    –Plans for quality improvement measures if a reduction in enrollment is requested (to maintain current grant funding).

    –Creates a systemic process to annually review community assessment data and adjust to on-going strategic planning as warranted.

    –Opens doors for communication and working collaboratively with community partners to provide quality services for children and families in the community.

***When* will each component occur?**
- An enrollment plan which will identify an expected date for full enrollment is due to the Office of Head Start within 90 days.
- Enrollment will be reported monthly to track how the plan is working.
- Enrollment data will be reviewed and discussed by all stakeholders

at the end of the current program year and prior to the start of the next program year to determine if adjustments need to be made.

Where **will the process take place?**
- Windy River Head Start is located within one early childhood education facility.
- All technical assistance and other work will be completed on-site or virtually (conference calls/Zoom meetings) per the program director's discretion/request.

How **will the necessary components occur?**
- The Head Start Training and TTA Specialist will facilitate a strategic planning session within two weeks on-site at the program with program staff as determined by the Director. Outcomes will be to determine a community assessment process, data sources, and community stakeholders. A timeline of the work and a framework for the enrollment plan will also be drafted.
- The enrollment plan will note considerations specific to the tribal community.
- The TTA Specialist will meet with the Program Director per set schedule to discuss progress, facilitate group discussions regarding analyzed data, explore program options, and assist in planning next steps.
- Follow-up meetings at the end of the program year and prior to the beginning of the next programming year will be planned with stakeholders to review progress and enrollment status.

—Nicole Terry

LISTENING CONCEPTUALLY AND CONTEXTUALLY

FOR PROCESS CONSULTANT DISCUSSION

1. In reading this case study and thinking about what it means to listen conceptually, what are the potential words/phrases that may need operating definitions? Why? How do you approach clarification or define meaning with the Client?
2. What does listening contextually mean to this case study: Listening underneath? Listening forward? Listening Across? Listening beyond? How is listening conceptually important to the criteria for success?
3. Is there an even greater importance in listening conceptually and contextually when working with peoples of different cultures? Why or why not?

2. Intense conflict in a community

Background. A United Church Congregation in Southwestern Ontario reached out regarding critical issues they were having with their leadership team. In conversation with them, it was discovered they are a small family-sized church with long historical roots within the community. The leadership team are mostly long-standing members with some newer ones. In the good old days, they called a full-time minister. Over time the position has declined to 10 hours per week. There is a sense of profound loss, shame, and disappointment. They have no Sunday school, no young people, and their own children and grandchildren do not attend church. The current minister, a recent graduate, has let it be known they will quit if there is no change. The Leadership Team talks over each other. They do not listen. They shout at one another to the point of frustration.

THE SECOND CORE COMPETENCY

PROCESS DESIGN

Why **are we doing this?** The congregation is in crisis. If they do not change the way they do things, they will surely cease. This starts with the Leadership Team becoming able to function with basic communication.

Who **plays what roles as we address this?** The Process Consultant will facilitate four sessions with the Leadership Team via Zoom, using the talking stick model created by Indigenous Ministers and Leaders.

The clergy had their own session with the Process Consultant in addition to participating with the Leadership Team.

The regional body of the denomination approved this intervention and is providing funding to make it possible.

What **criteria do we use to know that we succeeded?**
- The Process Consultant will observe behavioral changes when congregational leaders met.
- Leadership Team members will be able to affirm each other.
- Leadership Team members will express that they feel relief, less stress, and less grief.
- There will be a tangible sense of forward motion and possibility in the congregation.

When **do we wish this work to be completed?** In a three-month period, with a final meeting to follow.

Where **will this work take place?** All meetings will take place virtually.

How **will we proceed?**
- Four structured listening sessions with facilitated conversation, using a talking stick (or stone) methodology.
- A specific conversation with the pastor.
- The Process Consultant will also attend a Church Council

meeting after the structured listening sessions are complete. This is to observe and report—a means for the Leadership Team to also note if they are experiencing any changes.

- A final meeting with all involved to debrief on the experience and consider what might now be possible.
- A final and evaluative report will be generated to the regional body of the denomination.

—Eleanor Scarlett

FOR PROCESS CONSULTANT DISCUSSION

1. Can you identify the structure for listening in this case study? What would you affirm, adjust, or add?
2. Do you believe these activities will assist conceptual and contextual understanding? Why or why not?
3. What contextual clues would make you want to know more if you were facilitating these conversations? What words or phrases should you not assume you understand?
4. In addition to facilitating a talking stick conversation, what is important in the Process Consultant's role in helping the Leadership Team hear one another?
5. How do you think this scenario ends? Why? What would be important for it to have a successful outcome? What are some next processes this congregation likely faces should they begin to hear one another and begin to work together again?

The Third Core Competency

LISTENING ARCHITECTURALLY

Process Consultants bring their whole selves to the act of perceiving. In striking and holding a listening posture, Process Consultants attune all their senses to the speaker. They seek to be comprehensive as they gather and organize concepts and context and demonstrate understanding. Not until the Client says *Yes, you said it better than I did!* is it appropriate to bring insight or specific expertise alongside the Client as they partner to determine a scope and sequence for what happens next.

What happens next is listening at the architectural level. The Client is listening too. This type of listening draws the Client out in deciding what will be done to address their "it."

THE LISTENING POSTURE OF THE PROCESS CONSULTANT

Let's get a running start by reviewing the Core Competencies thus far:

THE THIRD CORE COMPETENCY

- Listening Actively and Comprehensively, the Process Consultant listens *to* the Client.

- Listening Conceptually and Contextually, the Process Consultant listens *for* the Client.

As we move to Listening Architecturally, we learn the Process Consultant listens *with* the Client. The Client has joined the listening. They are listening to themselves. The Client is now listening more fully to:

- Their underlying issue.

- The context in which they intend to address their underlying issue.

- Their own readiness to engage their "it."

- The action steps they will commit to take, with whom, and toward what end.

CLIENT	PROCESS CONSULTANT	ITERATION		
Articulates what we need to do and why	Listens Actively and Comprehensively	WHY	Right Brain	Listening to
Identifies what we are actually willing to do and why. Then:	Listens Conceptually and Contextually	WHY WHO	Right Brain	Listening for
• Who will do it	Listens Architecturally	WHO	Left Brain	Listening with
• What success criteria will guide them	Listens Architecturally	WHAT	Left Brain	Listening with
• When they will complete the work	Listens Architecturally	WHEN	Left Brain	Listening with
• Where the work will be done	Listens Architecturally	WHERE	Left Brain	Listening with
• How they will go about completing the work	Listens Architecturally	HOW	Left Brain	Listening with

Figure 4

The boxes in Figure 4, above, identify a flow from a place of immobility toward specific action. As the conversation shifts from "might do" to "will

LISTENING ARCHITECTURALLY

do," Client energy shifts along with it. Those on the Client's team who love to identify ideas (Right Brain) grow quieter and those who need a list of items to check off (Left Brain) begin engaging and creating those lists. This is especially true if everyone can see their input into the architecture of a process that will be followed. As a Process Design is built between the Client and the Process Consultant, Client alignment and commitment grows with it.

The good news here is that by asking the iterative questions *why, who, what, when, where,* and *how,* from the beginning, the Process Consultant and Client assemble the parts of a Process Design. They are already fostering alignment throughout the Client organization. Together, they assemble the process from the very first listening interaction. This is their key means for developing trust and being persuasive.[20]

If the Client expects plug and play items from the Process Consultant, it might not be a right fit.[21] Most plug and play items are actually technical, follow-this-method solutions for known problems or opportunities. However, the Process Consultant's vocation exists in the realm of adaptive moves, hunting for stepping stones and buried treasure in unmapped place alongside their Clients. They then make sense of and use what is learned.

Architectural listening is not exclusive to Process Consultation. Design Thinking and Agile methodologies also use Process Design elements. These methodologies expect original thinking that goes beyond previously established best practices, and design that occurs in collaboration with the Client. Consider this quote from Barry Overeem,[22] an Agile thought leader who pushes companies to do original architectural work when problem-solving and not just play copycat:

THE THIRD CORE COMPETENCY

> **Barry Overeem** · 2nd
> Unleashing Organizational Superpowers
> 3d · 🌐
>
> Organizations that suffer from Zombie Scrum like to follow standardized methods, well-defined frameworks, and "industry best-practices". To them, this feels more efficient than developing their own approaches.
>
> There are three big problems with "copying" from others like this:
> 1) Copying what works for one organization to another completely ignores the unique circumstances that enabled the solution to work for the original organization.
> 2) The very nature of complex systems means that there are no "models" or "best practices".
> 3) By simply copying the (supposed) result, organizations never develop the ability to learn that is essential to solving complex challenges.
>
> You can certainly find inspiration in solutions from other organizations. But instead of jumping straight to replicate their recipes, it's more helpful to create environments where people can learn and fail. Don't copy the plant, copy the soil it grew from.

Figure 5

Think about the difference between working with an architect to build a house versus working with a real estate agent to look at houses already built. Process Consultants are architectural, working with the Client to build process toward the Client's unique and contextual vision. Process Consultants are not real estate agents showcasing and selling what was already built elsewhere.

We now come to the specifics of listening architecturally.

Why, who, what, when, where, and *how* help any Process Consultant get started in designing a process with the Client. Using these questions is a stalwart and focusing mental discipline. This discipline not only builds a specific process, but it also breaks the overall Client intention into its respective parts so that almost anyone in the Client organization can follow or communicate about what is happening. Further, it specifically identifies any ongoing role a Process Consultant might play as the Client addresses their "it" — perhaps with process, perhaps in their specific area of expertise, and perhaps in arrangement with colleagues because additional expertise needs to be involved for the Client's success.

These iterative questions move progressively from general aspiration to specific action. Almost any resulting specific action in a Process Design can be written in just one or two sentences. Here is an example:

> *During this outbreak of COVID* (why), *the HR task force* (who) *is committed to further innovate and continue all leadership development training programs by moving them to an online environment* (what *and* where), *beginning the first week of August* (when). *The next email to you will contain instructions for virtual connection* (how).

Any specific action, such as the example above, will likely have subtasks. Subtasks are more granular actions that build toward the intended result and make it possible. It is preferable that the Client is a full participant in forming and mapping these subtasks, including who will do them and how it can be recognized that a task is complete. A Process Consultant should not attempt to form or map subtasks beyond their own level of expertise. Gaining specific answers to the iterative questions needs to be in the Process Consultant's toolbox, but highly detailed specific Project Mapping does not. The Client's knowledge and skill needs to be prominently displayed in the tasks and subtasks as one of the signs of their ownership to take specific and measurable action. Other experts, perhaps the Process Consultant's colleagues, can provide needed and timely expertise, especially where subtasks are concerned and neither the Client nor the Process Consultant have what is needed. Bringing the Process Design together through the posture of listening, articulating, and organizing is the consulting task and should not become diminished by the Process Consultant serving as both Facilitator and Subject Matter Expert.

Recognizing that there will often be a gap between what is needed and the Client and/or Process Consultant's skill, the Client may choose to call on a vendor or will ask the consultant to bring in a colleague(s) who holds the needed expertise. Examples of this may include:

- Developing Charts or Process Maps, especially those with task dependencies.
- Project management.
- Conducting and reporting on focus groups and individual interviews.
- Statistical analysis—whether qualitative or quantitative.
- Subject matter expertise to further advise the process, especially as adaptive moves are identified.

It is okay for one or more elements in a Process Design to be labeled as To Be Determined (TBD). When doing so it is important to include the steps by which the matter will be determined (*when, who, how*). TBD should not be used as a delay tactic.

The architectural stage is where passive-aggressive behavior, what Kim Stezala and I called "the Lieutenant Effect" in our paper *Wheel Forward or Spiral Downward*,[23] comes into play. The Lieutenant Effect causes harm to and limits impact of a process because a key player works behind the scenes to undermine the process.[24] They will say things like *We don't need outsiders*, or *We don't need to spend money on this. Let me take it over.* Often, it is because they are afraid their well-protected incompetence will be exposed, or because they were once an advocate for the very thing the process is addressing but their work went unheeded. Many a good Process Design loses its way if a lieutenant's whisperings remain hidden.

This form of passive aggression seldom surfaces and becomes visible in any immediate way. It operates behind the scenes and in context, usually after the Process Consultant leaves the room. Process Consultants are wise to expect the reality of the Lieutenant Effect, and to be prepared to notice it and name it so that it can be addressed early in the Process Design.

The Lieutenant Effect is one reason for the listening competencies of Process Consulting to be in place and to continue throughout the Client engagement. Listening architecturally does not mean the previous forms of listening cease. The listening competencies of the Process Consultant stack and build. They are not merely a sequence through which one moves.

CONCLUDING THOUGHT

Architectural listening moves from right brain to the left brain of the Client organization and back again, from the *why, who,* and *what* to the *where, when,* and *how*. The Process Consultant is the Corpus Collosum[25] of the Process Design, making sure the creative thinking can tie to the needed granular tasks that build toward a successfully completed process. Along the way, the Process Consultant pays attention to what can build and what will attempt to dismantle the process architecture.

Listening Architecturally
CASE STUDIES

1. Arts and anti-racism

Background. Arts Are Integral (AAI) is a medium-sized arts education non-profit organization with more than 30 years of service in a large city in the Midwest. The organization is at a critical moment of awareness and commitment regarding their inclusion and anti-racism commitments.

Three years ago, AAI established a diversity, equity, and inclusion task force, beginning a process of relationship and awareness building, learning, and engagement. The CEO and team members began to struggle to make their good intentions actionable and meaningful beyond tokenizing diversity efforts. They were seeking mindset changes and concrete learning and action to grow inclusiveness and anti-racism among staff, board leadership, partner organizations, and particularly with those served by their organization.

AAI is located in a county with nearly 30 percent BIPOC (Black, Indigenous & People of Color) residents while organizational leadership and board members are predominantly White. Approximately 50 percent of staff and almost all of those served by AAI are BIPOC. There is a call for a different future to better reflect the community through more inclusivity.

Marie, the CEO, reached out after attending a racial equity event where a Process Consultant was a speaker. Marie wanted to discover how their organization could move forward with making their inclusive intentions a reality. Together they created a process to collaboratively design an anti-racist framework for AAI.

PROCESS DESIGN

Why **is this being worked on (missional)?** Staff that identify as Black and/or Indigenous People of Color (BIPOC) shared with Marie and other leadership cabinet members that they experience a lack of safety within the organizational environment and when engaging with their partner organizations. AAI intends to work toward brave spaces marked by belonging. They believe this is critical both inside AAI and externally among partner organizations and community members.

Leadership cabinet members believe that their mission as an educational arts organization is rooted in racial equity commitments, but they aren't sure how to be anti-racist and combat anti-Blackness.

Who **is playing what role in the process?** Marie, CEO of the nonprofit organization, authorized the Process Consulting Agreement and its funding. Two

Process Consultants, a Black and a White woman, will serve as co-planners, thought partners, and facilitators.

The nonprofit's leadership cabinet will be integrally involved in the learning networks, planning and execution of the work. All staff will be informed and engaged throughout the process per the objectives of this work as decided by the leadership cabinet and CEO.

Informational updates will occur periodically with the Board of Trustees, co-planned by Marie and the Process Consultants, and led by Marie. Marie and the leadership cabinet member in charge of operations will be primary communicators with the Board of Trustees and staff. The Process Consultants and Marie will be primary communicators with leadership cabinet members, scheduling meetings, sharing minutes, and setting the scope and sequence together.

What criteria mark success? AAI desires a process of intentional, co-created systems building equity, inclusion, belonging, and an anti-racism framework, utilizing resources, models, and best practices as guides. Leadership cabinet members want to design and implement organization systems and practices with sustainable tools for leaders and teams to apply internally and with partner organizations. They do not want check-the-box, sit-and-get trainings; they want to build capacity, increase knowledge, and create an anti-racist framework to specify what they believe, why they believe it, how they will commit to anti-racism individually and organizationally.

Marie and the leadership cabinet members recognize the harmful effects of White supremacy in themselves, their relationships, and within systems. They are dedicated to decreasing harm, increasing inclusiveness, leading when needed, and getting out of the way as necessary.

Organizational leaders desire to grow systems of staff support and accountability, building the capacity of White- and BIPOC-identifying staff with spaces, systems, and structures to disrupt inequity in themselves, interpersonally, within the organization, and in partner organizations and systems.

Commitments toward the work of this Agreement in the next six months include creating an anti-racist framework, developing a plan to change organizational culture toward more inclusiveness and belonging, facilitating learning experiences that will lead toward shared understanding of racial oppression and its impact within AAI.

When **will this work be completed?** The Process Consultants will support AAI through six months of engagement with the CEO and leadership cabinet. They will also support the creation of a steering committee consisting of leadership cabinet members and staff to co-plan regular meetings, thought partner sessions, and facilitated team development opportunities to create the anti-racist framework.

Where **is this work being conducted?** This work primarily takes place virtually via Zoom due to COVID19 physical distancing requirements. Phone calls and email will be utilized as needed and appropriate throughout the process for planning purposes.

How **will the work proceed?** The Process Consultants will support the organization in learning about systemic racism in the arts nonprofit sector, utilizing industry-wide reports and data for learning and application.

The Process Consultants will utilize best practices of adult learning, anti-racism, equity and inclusion, design thinking, change theory, assets-based practices, adaptive leadership, group facilitation, program design and development, systems mapping, etc., as applicable and necessary throughout the process.

The Process Consultants and the core leadership cabinet will co-plan appropriate meetings, thought partner sessions, and facilitated team development opportunities over a six-month period. A staff planning, engagement, and communication plan will be co-created and iterated throughout the process, led by the CEO and leadership cabinet.

The team will utilize pertinent organizational historical documentation from the organization as necessary. Reflection on progress, learning, and clarifying commitments will be utilized throughout the process, and closing of the engagement will occur upon creation of the anti-racist framework.

NOTE: AAI's leadership cabinet members will also hold twice monthly leadership cabinet meetings to the scope of this Agreement, starting about one month into the engagement. The leadership cabinet members realize that they need time and space to do their own work, which consists of leadership development, trust building, growing understanding of systemic racism in the organization and nonprofit sector, change theory, and personal racial consciousness awareness building.

—Deanna Rolffs

FOR PROCESS CONSULTANT DISCUSSION

1. What architecture for a process do you find here? How do you think it emerges out of the Process Consultant's listening? What do you think is missing?
2. How does listening architecturally further clarify a Client's scope and sequence before, during, and after a Process Consulting engagement?
3. In reading this case study, what might be missing in the Process Design? How do you think the racial and other identities of the Process Consultants and Clients impact the goals? What questions might you ask to bring further clarity for the Client?
4. How and when might you include staff, board trustees, or partner organization during the design or implementation? What potential challenges do you foresee in the rollout of the anti-racist framework? How would you navigate those challenges to support the leadership cabinet and CEO?

2. Growth spurt for a sport

Background. The Wallyball Sports Council now has 500 chapters in three regions. Each region is its own 501I(3) and contributes out of chapter dues to fund a modest national office, also a 501I(3). In turn, the national office makes scholarships available for Wallyball coaches who are pursuing degrees in education or sports medicine. An international Wallyball Confederation is being explored.

A recent strategic plan that drew on input from all chapters and regions revealed a strong desire to launch an International Confederation, then begin the arduous process of lobbying to have Wallyball become an Olympic Sport. A Process Consultant was contacted because the governance system for the Wallyball Sports Council—even as a small sport compared with others—was bogged down, especially among the leaders and boards of the three regions. Without a leaner structure and streamlined form of governance, adding a lobbying effort to become an Olympic Sport was impossible. There was too much haggling over the rules of each competition, too much jockeying for influence among the regions, and too much dispute about how the Wallyball Sports council received and spent its money.

At the same time, the relaxed and fun culture of Wallyball participants meant that local sponsorship of tournaments, standardization of tournament rules, and increased professionalism of coaches and referees was needed. Without local ownership of a focused international effort, the sport was dead in the water.

How could they, as a growing sport, carry forward fun and passionate participation at the local level, while becoming more agile and responsive as a growing, international sport?

PROCESS DESIGN

Why **streamline a governance process?** The Wallyball Sports Council is an associational system looking to build an international layer. Chapters, Regions, the Wallyball Sports Council, and the fledgling International Wallyball Confederation will need to combine efforts toward the strategic end of becoming an Olympic-level sport. To achieve this ambitious outcome, a streamlined form of decision-making and action is desired.

Who **is involved and what are their roles?**
- Justeen Washington, the Wallyball Sports Council Executive Director, will oversee the Process. She will also coordinate with the task force to develop the International Wallyball Confederation.
- The cost to study and then streamline governance is funded jointly among the three regions with each regional director covering their cost for participation, as well as proportionately dividing the fees for a Process Consultant.
- The boards of each region and all chapter directors will be consulted and communicated with along the way.
- Parker Smith will serve as Process Consultant, facilitating a sequence of conversations that involve the three regional directors and Justeen Washington.

What **will we recognize as a successful effort?**
- We will develop an idealized governance system, followed by a comparison of how we govern now. This will reveal a map of "here to there" that we intend to complete within 18 months.
- Our governance system will require less time from all participants than it does currently, while increasing the frequency of communication between all levels.

- Our governance system will tie to the developing International Wallyball Confederation.
- We will have a greater confidence that we can build this into an Olympic-level sport.
- We will work our way into a new governance reality.

When **does this work need to be completed?** The intention of the task force developing the International Wallyball Confederation is to have the Confederation in place within two years. This effort to simplify the governance of the Wallyball Sports Council should be completed at least six months prior.

Where **is this work taking place?** While seeking counsel from all chapter directors, the primary work will be done within a series of structured conversations between the regions and the national office.

How **are we proceeding from here?**
- Dates for the structured conversations are being scheduled and are currently envisioned as two, two-day meetings at the national offices in Long Beach, California. These meetings are to be completed within six months.
- The first two-day meeting will be used to develop a task and sequence list. The status of each task will be tracked and reported on at the second two-day meeting. Any subsequent gatherings of this task force will be determined at the second meeting.

—Mark L. Vincent

FOR PROCESS CONSULTANT DISCUSSION

1. This case reveals a rather open-ended architecture for a process. How might that help or hinder the process?
2. Do you believe the process architecture adequately addresses the scenario described in the background? Why or why not?

3. What varying levels of control do you notice between chapters, regions, a national office, and a forming international confederation? How might that influence the architecture of a process?
4. What other issues do you notice beyond developing a governance structure? How might they come into play and how might the Process Consultant either incorporate them or hold them at bay? How might a Process Consultant identify whether they should be incorporated?

The Fourth Core Competency

LISTENING ADAPTIVELY

Listening adaptively becomes possible because of the listening posture of the Process Consultant. Assuming that posture requires intentional and conscious work.

> "But there is another kind of seeing that involves a letting go. When I see this way I sway transfixed and emptied. The difference between two ways of seeing is the difference between walking with and without a camera. When I walk with a camera I walk from shot to shot, reading the light on a calibrated meter. When I walk without a camera, my own shutter opens, and the moment's light prints on toy own silver gut. When I see this second way I am above all an unscrupulous observer . . .
>
> All I can do is try to gag the commentator, to hush the noise of useless interior babble that keeps me from seeing just as surely as a newspaper dangled before my eyes. The effort is really a discipline requiring a lifetime of dedicated struggle; it marks the literature of saints and monks of every order East and West, under every rule and no rule, discalced and shod...
>
> The world's spiritual geniuses seem to discover universally that the mind's muddy river, this ceaseless flow of trivia and trash, cannot be dammed, and trying to dam it is a waste of effort that might lead to

madness. Instead, you must allow the muddy river to flow unheeded in the dim channels of consciousness; you must raise your sights; you look along it, mildly, acknowledging its presence without interest and gazing beyond it into the realm of the real where subjects and objects act and rest purely, without utterance. 'Launch into the deep,' says Jacques Ellul, 'and you shall see.'"

—Annie Dillard, excerpts from *Pilgrim at Tinker Creek*, as published in *Devotional Classics*, Richard J. Foster and James Bryan Smith, eds.

The Listening Posture of the Process Consultant
- The Process Consultant strikes a whole-self listening posture and actively listens *to* the Client. They listen comprehensively.
- The Process Consultant helps the Client move into a listening posture also, listening with them for concepts and context as they describe their "it."
- The Process Consultant becomes a facilitative partner *with* the Client, listening with them as they design a process by which they will address "it," identifying what they need to do, what they are actually willing to do, who will do it, by when, and their criteria for success.
- The Process Consultant listens *within* and *beyond* the Client's current moment. The Client engages in action, followed by reflection that leads to the next actions. The Process Consultant listens adaptively, listening within and beyond the Client's capacity, helping them stay true to their process, assessing any amendment to the Process Design because of what the Client learns.

Adaptive listening, listening within and beyond:
- Is the ability to modulate one's listening throughout the Client

engagement, especially as a Client relationship begins and then a Process Design is formed.

- Is the ability to keep the *why*, *who* and *what* of a Process Design in front of the Client as the Client acts, learns, adapts, and then acts again.

- Is the ability to point beyond where the Client is arriving, toward what is appearing on the desired horizon now that the Client has moved.

CLIENT	PROCESS CONSULTANT	ITERATION		
Articulates what we need to do and why	Listens Actively and Comprehensively	WHY	Right Brain	Listening to
Identifies what we are actually willing to do and Why. Then,:	Listens Conceptually and Contextually	WHY WHO	Right Brain	Listening for
• Who will do it	Listens Architecturally	WHO	Left Brain	Listening with
• What success criteria will guide them	Listens Architecturally	WHAT	Left Brain	Listening with
• When they will complete the work	Listens Architecturally	WHEN	Left Brain	Listening with
• Where the work will be done	Listens Architecturally	WHERE	Left Brain	Listening with
• How they will go about completing the work	Listens Architecturally	HOW	Left Brain	Listening with
Acts — Reflects — Evaluates — Learns — Acts again	Listens Adaptively	WHY WHO WHAT	Right Brain	Listening within and beyond

Figure 6

Figure 4, shown earlier, did not have the bottom row now seen in Figure 6, above. Each box identifies the flow from a seeming stuck place toward specific action. As the conversation shifts from "might do" to "will do" Client energy shifts along with it. Those on the Client's team who love to identify ideas grow quieter and those who need a list of items to check off begin engaging and creating those lists. This is especially true if everyone can recognize their input in the architecture of a process that will be followed — the Process Design. As the Process Design is built together, alignment and commitment grow with it. Commitment and alignment make for a more effective process than when an initiative is decided from above and then handed down to people who must carry it out without opportunity to help form it.

The added bottom row identifies the generative or triple-loop learning process in which the Client engages as they move through the process of figuring "it" out.[26]

The Process Consultant now helps the Client remain focused on *why* they are engaged, *who* agreed to play what role, and *what* the criteria for success is as guardrails for evaluating, re-gauging and then re-engaging the work. Said differently, when the Process Consultant listens adaptively, they become less a third party, objective and outside observer. They become a participant, a co-learner. They become the Client's annex, a thought partner that is influencing and being influenced within the process.

Once again we ask, *How can any one person remember all of this information and incorporate it into a consistent listening posture?* It is a simple answer. We cannot, and even the most practiced and masterful Process Consultant cannot do it perfectly. We need Clients with an "it" to work through to join with us in the listening. We need colleagues who amplify and/or extend our capacity to bring value to the Client. We need to embrace ongoing adaptation so that we can learn from our mistakes, learn what we hoped to, and most of all, be surprised by what we discover.

Similarly, we cannot discover with the Client unless the Client trusts the process they helped to design. If they don't trust they will not take the next step. That next step sheds light just a bit further through the mist toward the next stepping stones on the way to an ever-further horizon. *The practiced ability to listen for, identify, and then point to those stepping stones is a key benefit the Process Consultant brings to the Client.* The Client now has the opportunity to creatively recombine their knowledge/expertise on those stepping stones, making discoveries that would not have been revealed otherwise. And they

LISTENING ADAPTIVELY

would not have stepped there at all without the Process Design to do so. *Stepping stones that lead to discoveries are of the highest value to the Client, even if they cannot see them yet, and even if they are not originally part of the criteria of success in the Process Design.*

Consider these examples:

X-rays were discovered when trying to build a better cathode ray tube. X-rays were not what was originally sought.

Charles Goodyear wanted to find a better way to stabilize rubber. His experiments yielded nothing, but an unintended combination of sulfur with rubber brought about the needed vulcanization so that rubber did not melt in heat nor crack in cold.

In the first example, the discovery was not at all what was intended or sought. In the second, the discovery did not come about by what was commonly understood as the means to get there (the Process Design). In both cases, something valuable came about for a single reason. In addition to *why, who, what, when, where,* and *how,* the person at the center of the story took time within their process to ask *What do I have here?* Those involved were willing to adjust their process accordingly. They were able to extract discovery. Their *how* could be changed in pursuit of their *why.*

The Process Consultant helps the Client build adaptive conversations like these into each stage of a Process Design. They help the Client have these adaptive conversations through the formula introduced in the second Core Competency of Listening Conceptually and Contextually.

- Here is why we are working together—a reminder of the mission.
- That is where we were.
- Here is where we are.
- This is what we are doing now.

To this we add the Adaptive Conversation:

- What do we have here? Shall we adjust anything in our process because of what we now have?
- There is where we go next. Identify next steps between now and the next stage in the process.

The first four Listening competencies make up the listening posture that the Process Consultant strikes and holds:

- Listening actively and comprehensively—developing a trusting relationship with the Client.
- Listening conceptually and contextually—developing the Client's own conceptual and contextual listening and their internal alignment.
- Listening architecturally—designing the Process with the Client.
- Listening adaptively—modulating to the Client and fostering adjustments to the process based on the Client's insight.

With these first four competencies the Process Consultant listens thoroughly and then articulates what they hear until the Client can say *Yes*. At the very end, when the Client is in the process to which they've committed themselves, the Process Consultant begins to point the way toward stepping stones and discovery, but even this is predicated upon intensive listening with the Client's *why* in mind.

The Helping competencies of the Process Consultant come into play when and only when these first four Listening competencies are actively in place.

Listening Adaptively
CASE STUDIES

1. Your benefits are changing

How do you tell your employees that their benefits plan is going to change? How do you convince them that taking away some of their very generous benefits, even a small portion, is going to be better for them in the long run, because it will help the company save money? Even if that is true, how do you communicate that in a way that is genuine and credible? You listen adaptively.

A large, family-owned business with more than 1,500 employees operates retail branches and warehousing operations in five states, serving a mix of businesses and consumers. The company was experiencing rising benefits costs, and the chief human resource officer had been charged with creating a plan for passing some of those increased costs on to employees.

The business is family-owned and run by members of the second and third generations, as well as key leaders from outside the family. The family places a high value on treating its employees with care and respect. The founder was legendary for his personable style, knowing every employee in every location by name and many long-time employees still remember him with fondness and respect.

Within this context of family values, the leadership knew that listening to employees would be an important first step in this change process. The company has a history of adaptive listening at key inflection points and that listening posture has yielded tangible results in the form of increased employee loyalty, even during several turbulent times in the company's 100-year history.

Listening to the leadership, it was clear that their care and concern for the employees is a key value and motivation in their decision-making, and they hoped for a strategy that would allow them to continue to care for employees while maintaining the financial sustainability of the company for the long-term. This became the criteria for the project's success—to find a way for both employees and company to believe they were "in this together," in the same way a healthy family looks out for the needs of each other. The Process Consultant worked with the Chief Human Resource Officer (CHRO) to design the scope of the listening engagement. The primary objective was to develop a strategy for increasing the amount that employees contributed to their company benefits plans, in a way that would be acceptable to employees. This strategy would include recommendations for how to implement that contribution increase and how best to communicate the plan to employees. In addition to the CHRO, the entire leadership team took an active role in hearing a summary of the listening findings and developing the strategy to move forward based on the learnings.

From experience, the leadership knew it would be important for someone from outside the company to conduct the interviews and focus groups. An objective outsider provides a layer of anonymity and reduces fear of any repercussions, particularly in discussing sensitive topics such as compensation, benefits, and employee morale.

The process was designed to approach the topic from a broad perspective, covering multiple subjects in the interviews and focus groups. The conversations began broadly by first asking about the employees' overall experience working with the company, what they liked, what they didn't like, and then moving to more specific components of what they valued about their work, including specific questions about the compensation and fringe benefits, and how those compared to other companies in the industry. The goal was to identify employees' "why"—their reasons for coming to work at this company, beyond just the paycheck and the fringe benefits.

Progressing through the early stages of listening—interviews conducted with a small selection of employees at all levels at each of the retail branches and focus groups comprised of customer-facing and warehouse employees (but no management)—it became apparent that this broader, values-based approach to listening will be key to the ultimate success of the company's strategy.

What emerged was a much broader picture of employee engagement than the original scope of the project called for. Because the leadership of the company understands the value of listening, and because they were willing to adapt and modulate the scope of the project based on early listening results, they gleaned valuable information about the culture of organization and how it was impacting employee morale. One key finding in the initial stages was that culture and employee morale differs significantly from one location to another, and the tone set by the branch manager predicted how healthy or dysfunctional each branch is, and these dysfunctions are likely the cause of significant process inefficiencies. While the company is in the early stages of implementing leadership training at the middle management level, these early learnings have caused it to place much more emphasis on this important intervention.

Additionally, employees reported that they value working for the company and that they view health benefits as just one of the reasons they choose to work for the company. They identify strongly with the company history and the values of the family owners. Even for those who work in locations that are not managed as well, there is a sense of pride and security in working for a company that has enjoyed long-term success. Their benefits package is also source of pride for them, and they understand it compares favorably with what other companies offer.

Based on these findings, the leadership shifted its strategy from cutting benefits to improving culture and efficiency, recognizing that in the long run, these efforts will likely yield greater Return On Investment (ROI) than passing health care costs along to employees. This shift in strategy yielded growth for the company and improved employee loyalty.

How did adaptive listening benefit the Client? First, by designing an adaptive approach, as opposed to adhering rigidly to the original scope, the Process Consultant heard things the Client was not looking for, and those things turned out to be the most important learnings. Had the process doggedly clung to the original research objective, the Client would have marched along to certain failure. Even if employees knew their benefits package was more generous than others and they likely would have accepted a cut, the adaptive listening approach uncovered a strategy that resulted in a win for the company and its employees. By putting the organizational value of employee loyalty at the forefront, ahead of the original objective of reducing a benefit package, leadership was able to adapt its strategy.

Second, the Client and the Process Consultant agreed to look beyond a presenting issue of short-term monetary gain. This enabled them to shift from a negative strategy (subtracting something from employees) to something additive, enhancing the total work experience for all employees, which has led to greater loyalty and productivity gains that have far outpaced the cost savings of cutting benefits.

—Kay Edwards

FOR PROCESS CONSULTANT DISCUSSION

1. Identify *why*, *who*, *what*, *when*, *where*, and *how* elements for a Process Design from the above story.
2. Where along the way was the adaptive question "*What do we have here?*" being asked?
3. Is it a successful process if an outcome and action is altogether different than originally intended? Why or why not?
4. When is it appropriate for a Process Consultant to challenge the purpose of a project and focus on a point "beyond the horizon" that the Client may not yet see? How might the Process Consultant do this?

2. Running a business in wartime

Background. The NGWAVE Building Construction Company LTD, is situated in the Northwest Region (NWR) of Cameroon. Established in 1998, it constructs houses on demand as well as others for rent or lease. NGWAVE is owned by a group of construction engineers with 100 employees and three branches or extensions within the NWR.

The entire NWR is currently challenged by civil war that has lasted more than five years. The war led to people migrating to other parts of the country, which resulted in fewer available workers, fewer customers, and a smaller business development pipeline. Also, due to insecurity and lockdowns, the employees of this company who remain do not turn up for work regularly.

The proprietors of NGWAVE cherish their company and want to keep it alive and growing. Consequently, they seek the services of a Process Consultant to journey with them, their workers, and the stakeholders in a quest to find a way forward to revive their Company and ensure its growth.

PROCESS DESIGN

Why **are we engaged in this?** Continuity and the future of the NGWAVE Construction Company is uncertain and the proprietors are anxious about the prevailing situation. Measures to prevent a disastrous end of this enterprise have not been identified, explored, and adopted. To respond to this precarious situation, the owners want to put alternative plans and strategies in place that can move the business forward. This revival and growth plan is required to be in place by June of next year as they are unsure of how much longer the current war will last.

THE FOURTH CORE COMPETENCY

Who **plays what role as we engage in adaptive conversation about this?** The proprietors of NGWAVE Company intend to review their belief systems and problem-solving approach, while being open to embracing new ways and opportunities as they decide on what to do to revive and grow their business.

- The proprietors will collaborate with their management and technical teams, workers, and stakeholders for insights, understanding, cooperation, and buy-in.
- The Process Consultant will facilitate the discussions among and between the proprietors, management and technical teams, workers, and stakeholders.
- The Process Consultant will listen and engage them in action, then further reflect on the actions taken to identify where and what adjustments are or may be required. Gaining clarity and making adjustments will lead the proprietors, teams, workers, and stakeholders to engage in new actions that align with the options and strategies considered best to revive and grow their company.
- The proprietors, teams, workers, and stakeholders will be assisted by the Process Consultant to assess and adopt necessary amendments resulting from the lessons learned that will enhance their decision making.
- The proprietors of NGWAVE Company will assume the payment of all the expenditures related to the entire process.
- The Company secretariat, supervised by the project manager, will ensure smooth communication to and from all parties involved.

What **criteria will we consider in order to know that we succeeded?**

- Establish and seal a revival and growth plan by the end of June, next year.
- Adopt specific and well-defined activities, options, and strategies.
- Ensure that a good relationship exists between the Process Consultant and members of the company, and that a Process Design has been formed.

- Ensure that the proprietors and all parties involved are satisfied, happy about, and committed to the decisions made.

When do we wish this work to be completed?
- Beginning in January, the Process Consultant will meet monthly with each involved group as indicated by the schedule drawn with the management team to discuss and adopt proposals towards company revival and growth.
- By the end of March, the first draft of the road map towards concrete strategies, options and plans with the Process Consultant will completed.
- In April and May, feasibility studies where indicated will be completed.
- During May and June, any adjustments made will be documented and a final execution plan will be updated and established.
- By the end of June, the proprietors of NGWAVE Company will have a complete document detailing the actions and way forward for their company.

Where will this work be conducted?
The venue for the meetings and deliberations will be the La Verna Spiritual Centre, Nkwen in Bamenda. The environment is conducive, convenient, secure, accessible, and close to the Company's headquarters.

How will this work be conducted?
- The Process Consultant will draw up and sign an Agreement with the proprietors on the work and payment modalities.
- A sequence of activities will be established. The Process Consultant will meet with the proprietors, management team, technical staff, technical team, and stakeholders at designated times.
- In the monthly meetings with the various groups of people, the Process Consultant will listen as they share their ideas and

proposals on how to resolve the prevailing challenges. Questions will be asked for clarity of meaning and context to enhance a broader and shared understanding. The Process Consultant will ensure that assumptions, prejudgments, and miscommunications are avoided or resolved if they creep in. This will keep the conversation focused on the real situation.

- Key questions will be asked that will enhance reflection that can inspire better decisions. The questions may also help the proprietors, employees, and stakeholders to be flexible in adapting and adjusting to new ways and new ideas that can lead to the improvement, revival, and growth of the company.

- The Process Consultant, the proprietors, and all the parties involved will ensure that the stipulated timelines are duly respected.

- The implementation of the revival plan is envisaged to begin no later than the end of July.

- Follow up evaluation and documentation of lessons learned will take place in October and adjustments made accordingly to ensure the continuity of the company's mission.

Listening adaptively. The Process Consultant sets out to accompany the Client and in companionship offers them help to identify, accept, and adjust their way of thinking, beliefs, and actions to the actual reality as they work towards transformation. In this journey, the Consultant listens to get a full grip of the core and buried meaning of what the Client is saying while triggering them to keep in touch with the real situation without getting stuck on prefixed ideas.

—Lilian Vernyuy

LISTENING ADAPTIVELY

FOR PROCESS CONSULTANT DISCUSSION

1. In a setting where the Process Consultant works with so many groups of people, what challenges can they face and how can these be managed?
2. How might adaptive listening be useful in volatile and uncertainty-filled scenarios like this one?
3. Looking at the process followed by the Process Consultant, proprietors, and other collaborators, what are the strengths of the process? How do you see adaptive listening being integrated? What additional ideas can be added to improve and make this process more complete and successful?
4. What additional skills could the Process Consultant and the Client consider when working in a war-torn situation?

HELPING

The Fifth Core Competency

HELPING: CLIENT-CENTERED

Some define consulting as being paid to give advice. On occasion, if the advice perfectly matches the openness of the Client to receive it, their actual need for it, and their readiness to put the advice to use, that advice might be understood as Helping. A problem, however, is that a perfect match rarely happens. A larger problem is that this type of consulting centers on the Consultant rather than on the Client. An even bigger problem is that neither the Consultant nor the Client are Listening or Learning. In the dispensing advice form of consulting:

- The Consultant tells and the Client does or does not.
- The Consultant says what they know, and the Client offloads their responsibility to learn by relying on the Consultant's expertise (or ignoring it).

The advice-dispensing style of consulting might work when a technical change is involved—a known solution for a known problem, and when the match between Consultant and Client is perfect. This "I will sell you what I

THE FIFTH CORE COMPETENCY

know" form of consulting might work when a product is offered — a package the Client is expected to adopt, and there are few to no complicating factors.

But if consulting is defined as collaboratively considering a process for helping where problem and solutions have unknown factors, then both Consultant and Client must engage listening before helping so that learning may emerge.

- The Process Consultant actively listens to the Client and helps the Client to actively listen—to self, to others, to context, to data, to possibilities, to insight, to wisdom.[27]
- The Process Consultant exercises curiosity and deep thinking, and the Client joins them in partnership to discover, step onto, and then utilize the next stepping stones toward their mission.

Process Consulting works when adaptive changes are involved—possible solutions for newly defined opportunities or challenges. Process Consulting works when a process is enjoined—a set of steps through which the Process Consultant and Client patiently and persistently adapt. Helping is centered around the Client who is joined by the Process Consultant.

Consider Robert R. Carkhuff's longstanding and highly respected work, *The Art of Helping*.[28] The Helping model, as shown in Figure 7 below, is distilled to its simplest level.

PHASES OF HELPING

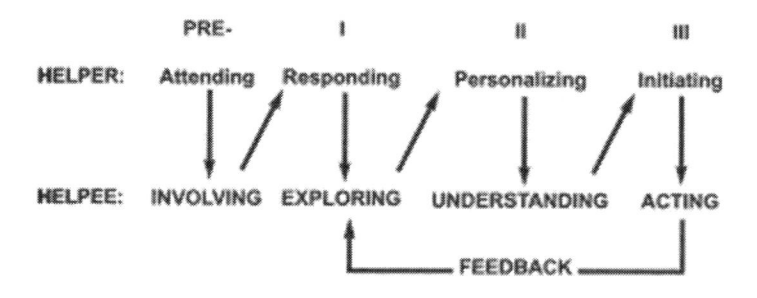

	PRE-	I	II	III
HELPER:	Attending	Responding	Personalizing	Initiating
HELPEE:	INVOLVING	EXPLORING	UNDERSTANDING	ACTING

FEEDBACK

Figure 7

HELPING: CLIENT-CENTERED

Carkhuff's model is used primarily in counseling, therapy, and social work scenarios. It can also apply to Process Consulting. The right-hand column in Figure 8 below shows how the Helping Model translates to Organizational Development and Client work. The Helper is the Process Consultant and the Helpee is the Client. Posing iterative questions, facilitating Process Design, engaging with the Client as they work through their process, and then assisting in the distillation of adaptive moves (Process Findings) and actions, are the Helping modes of the Process Consultant.

PHASES OF HELPING

	PRE-	I	II	III
HELPER:	Attending	Responding	Personalizing	Initiating
HELPEE:	INVOLVING	EXPLORING	UNDERSTANDING	ACTING

FEEDBACK

The Phases of Helping in Organizational Development

Pre-
- Iterative Questions

I
- Process Design

II
- Process Engagement

III
- Process Findings and Actions

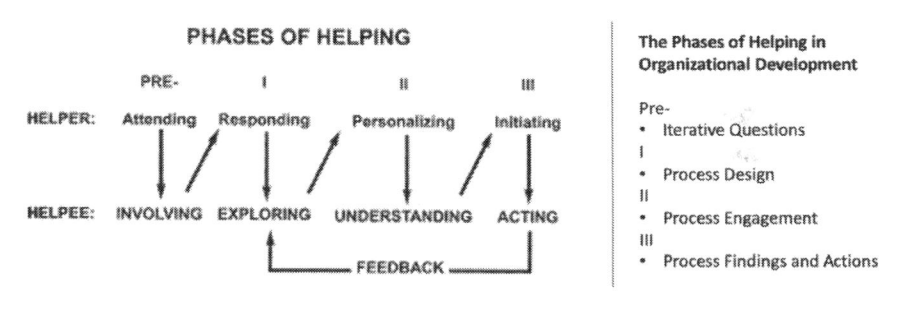

Figure 8

Process Consulting is not consultative help as a mode for research and reporting. Research can help a Client, but research can also be sold to the Client without ever making a personal connection.

Process Consulting is not knowledge contracting or selling expertise. A contractor can help the Client, but a contract can also be sold to the Client by filling out a requisition order.

Consider this definition of the Client-centeredness in Process Consulting developed by Kim Stezala, CEO of the Society for Process Consulting: "Client-centered consulting is wholly constructed and implemented such that every decision places the Client at the center, building *their* capacity to flourish."

Process Consultation is helping that comes alongside and joins in the labor of figuring the Client's "it" out:

THE FIFTH CORE COMPETENCY

- In partnership with the Client.
- At the Client's request.
- According to the Client's definition of success.
- In the Client's context.
- With the Client's confidence that it will make a difference.

The Core Competencies of Listening enable this trusting and Client-centered relationship to develop so that a Helping partnership is formed.

The Process Consultant needs to know that this trusting relationship is in place. So does the Client. It cannot be assumed. One way to know whether a trusting relationship is forming, or at least has the potential to form, is to find out if the following is in alignment:

- The *Helping message* the Process Consultant offers. To whom are you offering the value proposition?
- The *location within the organization where helping will take place*. With whom will your service be rendered?
- The *locus of authority where the decision to use the Process Consultant's help rests*. Who will make the decision to retain the Process Consultant's service?

Alignment[29] does not mean identical or unified. It means *lined up together*. This is the "center" around which Client work takes place. Players within the Client organization need to all be in the same conversation at the same moment of Client development so that a trusting and helping relationship can be developed.

Building on the above section, when developing the *who* section of a Consulting Agreement, among the *who* questions the Process Consultant asks are:

HELPING: CLIENT-CENTERED

- Whose decision is it whether we can do this work together?
- Who will be paying for this?
- Who will supervise this work?
- Who needs to be consulted as we put this together?
- Who is responsible for communicating with everyone involved throughout our Process?

This helps the Process Consultant discover if they are talking to all the organizational players involved. Is there someone else who holds decision making power or purse strings that could make the whole thing collapse if they are not in the conversation? If such a person is not sold on the mission and benefits of the work, then it quite possibly could not happen at all, or be severely limited in impact. The further out of alignment (the less centered) the conversations are with the locus of decision-making authority, the harder it is for the Process Consultant to be in a place to fully listen and then to offer competent help that is centered around the Client.

We invite you to a three-round exercise in mapping how centered a Client interaction is.

ROUND ONE—With your own consulting practice in mind place three dots on Figure 9.[30]

- The *Helping message* the Process Consultant offers. To whom are you offering the value proposition? Where do you find them in the Figure 9 diagram? Place a dot there.
- The *location within the organization* where helping will take place. With whom will your service be rendered? Put a dot on the diagram that represents them.
- The *locus of authority* where the decision to use the Process Consultant's help rests. Who will make the decision to retain the Process Consultant's service? Place a dot for them.

THE FIFTH CORE COMPETENCY

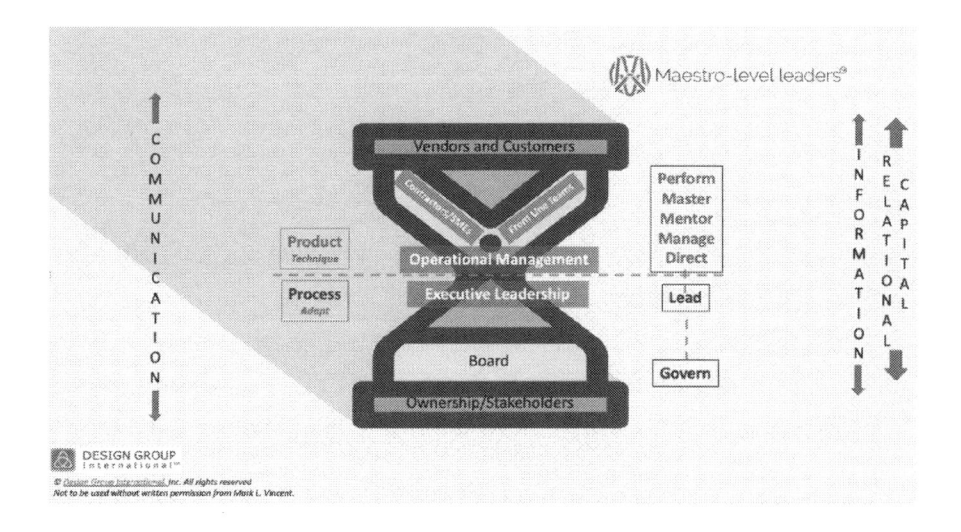

Figure 9

ROUND TWO—Complete the exercise again with a successful Client engagement in mind. Where would each dot be placed considering the same three questions? You might wish to use a different color.

ROUND THREE—Complete the exercise with an unsuccessful Client engagement in mind. Where do the dots land this time? Again, consider using a different color so all three rounds remain visible.

When you have completed the exercise, ask yourself:
- What do you observe about the closeness or separation of your dots in each round?
- Why do you think this is?
- What would you like to do with your observation(s)?

Now, let's share a couple of examples. In these examples, the Process Consultant can quickly see that this exercise is not about trying to bring the dots closer together. It is about knowing where they are so that what it takes to foster a Client-centered alignment becomes evident.

In the first example (Figure 10), the Helping message is primarily pitched to an operational manager such as a COO or HR Director (dot 1). The work is carried out with line workers, e.g., a training workshop, or perhaps as fact-finding interviews (dot 2). The actual decision to be made about retaining the Consultant appears to be with a hands-on Board (dot 3).

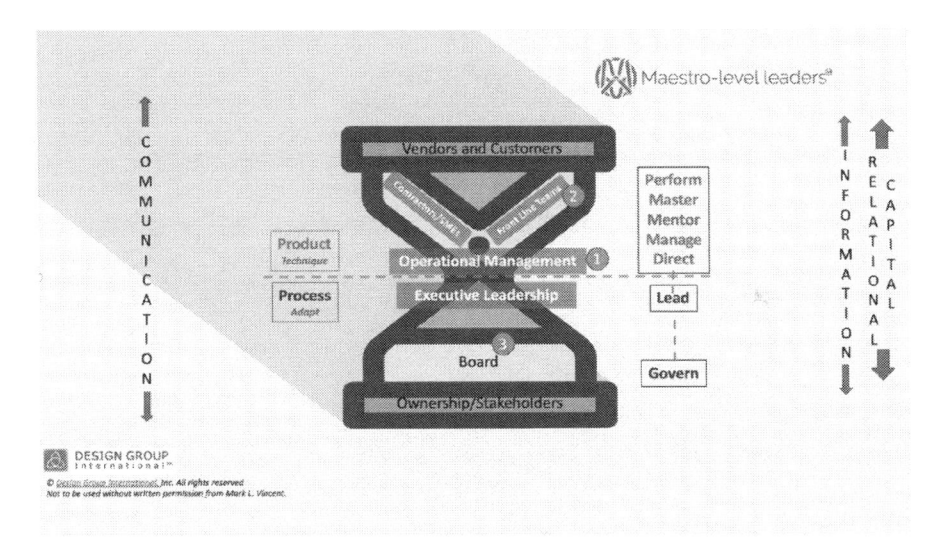

Figure 10

In the second example (Figure 11), the Helping message is primarily pitched to the Executive Director or CEO (dot 1). The work is carried out with operational management, e.g., executive coaching (dot 2). The actual decision to be made about retaining the Consultant in this case is with a Board, perhaps because the Board mandated the Executive Leader to do something to rescue the career of an Operational Manager (dot 3).

THE FIFTH CORE COMPETENCY

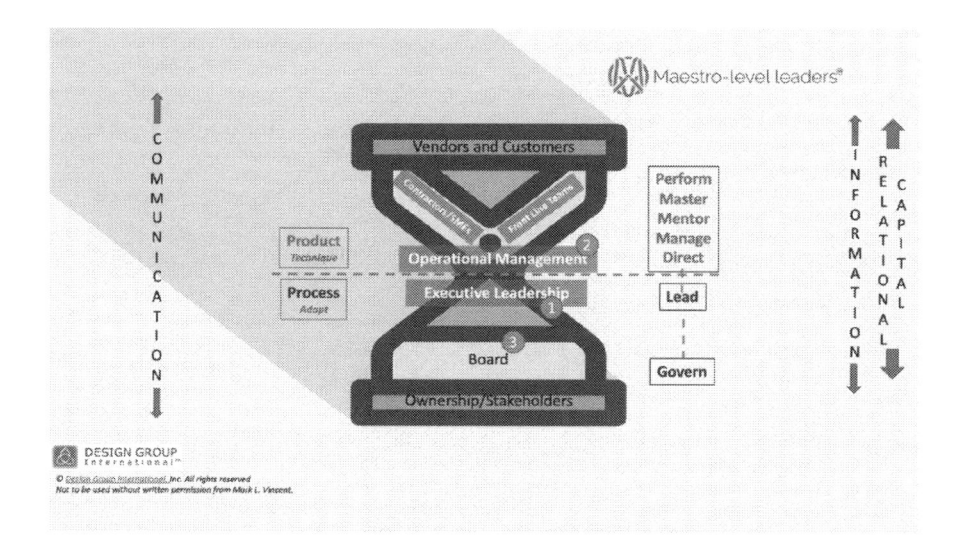

Figure 11

CONCLUDING THOUGHT

Helping that is centered around the Client is also Helping centered *in* the Client. The Process Consultant maintains a focus on the Client's objectives while fleshing out where within the Client organization the process will take place from start to finish. The Process Consultant also discovers whether the Client has organizational alignment—its own centeredness—to successfully complete the work.

Helping: Client-Centered
CASE STUDIES

1. Major donor relationships

Background. Thriving Tomorrow is a Midwest nonprofit organization dedicated to youth engagement and enrichment. For the past 15 years, the founder, Tom, has been leading the organization and developing relationships with a significant number of long-time donors, volunteers, and an eight-member Board of Directors. However, with Tom's recent passing, there is a void in leadership and a stall of donor cultivation with both existing donors and new connections to the mission.

The newly appointed Executive Director, Emily, had volunteered with Thriving Tomorrow for several years. She is a visionary and collaborative leader with a strong background in early childhood education, but has little fundraising experience. Furthermore, as with many nonprofits in the region, Thriving Tomorrow experiences significant staff turnover within its one-person Development Department. Currently, Emily is without a Development Director to manage the organization's appeals, annual fund, and donor relationships, but has been able to lean on the Board of Directors and long-time Marketing Director for assistance when needed.

With a fresh perspective and collaborative approach, Emily rallied the team and Board around her new vision, to elevate the mission and grow the organization from $3 million to $9 million within the next 10 years. A strategic plan has been affirmed, and Emily's next steps are to focus on cultivating major donor relationships and hiring a new Development Director. Emily began by attending a local workshop to learn more about how to build major donor relationships. While a Subject Matter Expert in the field, the presenter is a Process Consultant in her approach. After the workshop, Emily approached the presenter and expressed her need for help to build off Tom's great work and nurture major donors. The Process Consultant invited her to coffee to listen and learn more about Emily's needs. The following Process Design resulted.

PROCESS DESIGN

Why **are we doing this?** With a transition in leadership and Emily's willingness to adopt new, innovative processes, Thriving Tomorrow is poised for growth. Although Emily acknowledges her shortcomings—lack of fundraising experience, low confidence in cultivating major donor relationships, and currently no support from a Development Director—she is willing to invest the time and resources to build a solid foundation for fundraising strategy that will elevate the nonprofit.

While she searches for a Development Director, Emily needs a partner to help build a culture of generosity focused on the following key areas: building a compelling Case for Support, reconnecting and deepening relationships with major donors, and engaging the Board of Directors to support the organization's limited bandwidth.

Who **plays what role as we address this?** As the Process Consultant and Emily meet initially, the following were discovered in the discussion.

- **Making Decisions:** The Executive Director, in partnership with the Board of Directors, are the final decision makers.
- **Creating the Plan:** In collaboration, the Executive Director and Process Consultant will architect the generosity plan.
- **Doing the Work:** In collaboration, the Executive Director, Development Director (when hired) and Marketing Director will implement the plan and cultivate the major donor relationships.
- **Supervising:** The Executive Director will supervise the crafting of the Case for Support with the Marketing Director and Development Director (when hired).

- **Consulted Along the Way:** Because of their strong relationships with major donors, the Board of Directors will be consulted along the way.
- **Paying for It:** Thriving Tomorrow, the nonprofit organization, will pay for the services.
- **Handling Communications:** The Executive Director will handle communications with the current staff and Board of Directors by updating individuals about the process and next steps.

What criteria will mark success? Through the collaborative work between the Executive Director, Board of Directors, new Development Director (when hired), and Process Consultant, Thriving Tomorrow will begin to grow a culture of generosity by:

- Building a Case for Support and confidently articulating the mission and needs of the organization.
- Laying a solid foundation and understanding of fundraising strategy.
- Co-creating a three-year generosity plan to identify, cultivate, solicit, and steward major donor relationships.
- Establishing efficient practices for cultivating and developing major donor relationships.
- Instilling the confidence and understanding of how to build the culture of generosity into the organization's culture.
- Increasing the engagement of the Board of Directors and inviting their skillsets and networks to the table.

When do we wish work to be completed? Investing adequate time and resources to elevate the organization's fundraising efforts is top priority. The first 30 days will focus on building the Case for Support and engaging the Executive Director, Marketing Director, and Board of Directors in the process through a series of interactive workshops.

The next 90 days will be used to develop a three-year generosity plan, focused on cultivating major donor relationships and building a strong culture of generosity. The final generosity plan, co-created in partnership with the Executive Director, Development Director (when hired), and Process Consultant, will be presented to the Board of Directors at the end of the 90-day period.

Where **is the work being conducted?** The work will be conducted in a virtual setting with the Executive Director, as Emily has the flexibility to work virtually in her role. Board meetings will be conducted in Thriving Tomorrow's main office in Springfield, Illinois.

How **is the work proceeding?**

- **Design the process:** The Process Consultant and Executive Director met to develop the process at designing the generosity plan and reconnecting major donors to the organization's mission. The Executive Director discussed that the board has a variety of skill sets and relationships that can be tapped.

- **Listening Sessions:** To understand the organization's strengths, complexities, and culture, the Process Consultant begins the partnership by conducting individual listening sessions with the Executive Director and Board of Directors. Throughout this exercise, the Process Consultant poses pointed questions: *What does fundraising mean to you and how can you help? If a donor gave a $1 million unrestricted gift, how would it be used toward the mission?* Throughout these one-on-one connections, the Process Consultant listens with an open mind. Asking powerful questions and actively listening helps the Process Consultant build rapport and trust with the Executive Director and Board. But most importantly, the Process Consultant is able to unearth diverse perspectives, tap into individual skillsets and passions, collect new ideas, and listen to the wisdom within the organization, all of which help unlock unique solutions and contributions to the generosity plan.

HELPING: CLIENT-CENTERED

- **Collective Insights:** After the listening sessions are complete, the data, quotes, and insights are compiled, and the Executive Director and Process Consultant review the findings including skills, words, phrases, ideas, and wisdom that are uncovered. This helps everyone, including the Process Consultant, develop a deeper understanding of the organization and strengths in the room. By sharing the compiled insights, the leadership and Process Consultant learned about the perspectives of the board, including their understanding of fundraising and of the network of donor relationships.

- **Interactive Workshops/Fundraising Training:** To provide new learning experiences, build leadership capacity, and equip the Executive Director and Board with a clear understanding of fundraising and culture of generosity, the Process Consultant facilitates interactive workshops and fundraising training sessions in the next two Board meetings. The two-way conversations uncover new learnings and capacities from each person involved: board, Executive Director, and Process Consultant. Through these sessions, the organization's leaders and Process Consultant learn more about their specific Case for Support, skill sets and passions, the organization's fundraising philosophy, and new ideas to build the culture of generosity.

- **Tools/Aids:** Throughout the entire partnership, the Process Consultant will transfer knowledge and introduce specific fundraising tools and aids to help the Executive Director and Board better understand fundraising, building a culture of generosity, and the overall goals of the organization. The first tool presented is the Nonprofit Lifecycle Model, which shows where the organization stands currently and provides insights into the next steps for growth and elevation. The Process Consultant also uses a Case for Support storyboard sheet to walk the Executive Director,

Development Director, Marketing Director, and Board through the specific elements of the important document that will be used in donor meetings to express the needs of the organization. Finally, to help the Executive Director and future Development Director stay organized and cultivate major donor relationships, a strategic major donor plan chart and process is created by the Executive Director, Development Director and Process Consultant. The Executive Director and Development Director will work together to practice their process.

- **Co-Create Generosity Plan:** The Executive Director, new Development Director, and Process Consultant will use the information and input gathered throughout the entire partnership to create a generosity plan to ensure that that the founder's donor relationships are continually cultivated, new major donor relationships are identified and deepened, and a strong culture of generosity has been developed across the organization. This involves understanding donors' interests, what motivates them to give, what their wealth capacity is, and developing a sequence of communications and meetings to heighten engagement. The Process Consultant provides a framework to create the plan. The Executive Director and Process Consultant work together to design the overall goals and objectives of the generosity plan based on all the learnings thus far.

- **Activate the Board:** The Executive Director activates the engagement of members of the Board, based on all her learnings to date, with assignments to help with the fundraising efforts and building a strong culture of generosity. Based off their individual skillsets and level of comfortability, the Board begins to identify, cultivate, solicit, and steward major donors and be part of the fundraising process. The fundraising practices learned, tools, aids, and focus on major donor development becomes part of each Board meeting's agenda.

—Gretchen Colón

FOR PROCESS CONSULTANT DISCUSSION

1. What critique would you offer for the above Process Design?
2. Helping that is Client-centered is centered both on the Client and in the Client. Returning to Figure 9, where would you place the three dots in this case study?
3. How was Helping constructed and being played out?
4. How was trust built in the initial interaction between Emily and the Process Consultant at the workshop and the coffee shop conversation afterward? What types of actions or conversations would have changed this trust creation?

2. College troubles

New Day University celebrates its 75th anniversary in the new year. After a long-serving (17 years) president retired, a new president was appointed who had been trained as a lawyer and had not previously served in an academic institution. This is a non-traditional background for a college president, which meant that even before the new person started, they were already being looked upon with suspicion from the university community who did not see the president as "one of their own."

The new president understood that many challenges lay ahead. Because academic administration was a new endeavor for the president, it came with a realization that there was an industry-specific language he would need to learn. There was also little common experience between him and the university community that would aid communication and further build on common ground and experience. In addition, the words of the board who appointed him were recorded in his mind: *We need to change the culture and deal with the dysfunctional teamwork.* At the same time, after successfully serving as the CEO of a large hospital for 15 years, he felt he had some experience that would easily transfer to the new setting as he introduced ideas and concepts.

The university is at a crossroad. The economic viability model for higher education is changing, and the board did not feel the university was well prepared to adapt and innovate. The board also noticed that for the last few years, the past president's cabinet had served more as a "preserving and work as usual" entity with little thought given to the changing landscape. The whole institution seemed to be following the maxim, *Thou shall do things the way we have always done it before.*

Over his long tenure, the retiring president served the institution wholeheartedly and brought much-needed stability. Yet, in the last few years, he had shown characteristics of being tired, and he began working out of a maintenance mode until his retirement. This last period of his tenure began to be characterized by stagnation and conflict. No new programs were initiated. Several programs closed. The president's cabinet spent less and less time working and relating to each other and mainly retreated to the safety of their divisions. Each area was looking out primarily for themselves and the needs of their staff at the expense of the university's overall needs. An example? The question *What is best for the university?* became *What is best for the Student Life Division?* Although questions of this nature do not always need to be an either/or, the lack of maintaining the focus on the broader context was a significant challenge.

The outgoing and incoming presidents overlapped by several weeks. After attending his first cabinet meeting as an observer, the newly appointed president found himself wondering what he had gotten himself into.

The first part of the meeting had focused on the upcoming Higher Education Council visit for the accreditation of the institution. The conversation held so many acronyms he felt he had no idea what they were talking about.

HELPING: CLIENT-CENTERED

In the middle of this technical and acronym-laden discussion, significant infighting among the vice-presidents broke out, each one defending their department with the outgoing president publicly scolding several participants. The president also raised his voice and shouted over the conversation.

Each day of this overlapping period brought greater understanding of problem areas identified by the board. As part of his orientation and intent to get to know and learn about the university, he spent hours listening to various leaders and staff. He began to observe a pattern. The complaints he heard were all similar: *We are not appreciated. We are not consulted. We are just informed of decisions and not invited to participate. There is a lack of accountability. The persons in my area are working hard while the other divisions are wasting a lot of time!*

As the new president reflected on what he was learning, he observed that few people mentioned issues of race and intercultural competence. Approximately 20% of the university's staff were people of color, while the student population was predominantly (98%) Caucasian. It was clear to him that many of the problem issues and interpersonal conflicts were most likely rooted in a lack of intercultural competence and not performance problems as they were being described.

It reminded him of when he started working as a hospital CEO years ago. He had found a similar situation there and it had taken years of intentional work and culture change to move forward and for the hospital community to feel positive about it. He could begin to see a road forward for the university, but realized the road would be both long and bumpy.

The new president began to outline a working plan. His top priorities would be to develop a cohesive leadership team and to create a new culture, and he understood these goals were interconnected. The organizational culture needed to reflect shared assumptions.

The new president also understood that his behavior was critical and needed to reflect and embody the change he wanted to bring. He knew that it is typical for organizational members to get information about their leaders' priorities, values, and beliefs by simply observing where that leader spends their time, not just by what they say. Staff members would take their cues from his behaviors. He would need to behaviorally demonstrate the needed values and culture. This was important because intentionally or unintentionally, the president's cabinet members were reflecting the fatigued behaviors of the retiring president.

He was committed to reinforcing the desired organizational culture through his behavior, continually defining and clarifying expectations, setting clear accountability lines, and using opportunities created by staff transitions to hire faculty and staff whose value systems matched what was needed. He had studied the university's values and foundation as stated in the organizational documents, and they were extremely strong and powerful. Part of the task ahead was calling people to be the type of people and place that the organizational documents called everyone to be.

A "return to our values" was an essential component of his work and plan. He was coming in not to change the organization, but in a sense, to call the organization to live up to its potential and the vision it had already outlined.

The new president had two goals; to develop a cohesive leadership team and to change the organization's culture. He began to outline his approach for developing the team. He wrote that he would know when he would accomplish was he was looking for when he would have *a cohesive management and leadership team that will lead to (1) a smoother process through defined roles and objectives, (2) a team in which creativity would flow openly because of diverse talents and gifts that each person brings to the group, (3) a team in which each member would have an increased sense of individual autonomy and (4) where all felt safe to express out-of-the-box ideas, sharing their opinions freely and safely.*

As he thought of the organizational culture, he also began outlining specific characteristics of a healthy and functional culture. He wrote: *Our culture will(1) be one in which managers work in a collaborative way as a Cohesive Leadership Team, (2) a culture of clarity through effective and systematic communications systems, (3) a culture of excellence, (4) a culture of affirmation, (5) a culture with a strong faith development and identity, (6) a place known for the*

HELPING: CLIENT-CENTERED

Quality of Living for Residents, which is highlighted (resident-focused), (7) a place where people want to work, and (8) a place open to innovation.

One late afternoon, when he felt he was ready, he picked up the phone to talk with a Process Consultant he had drawn upon previously when CEO of the hospital . . .

—Carlos Romero

FOR PROCESS CONSULTANT DISCUSSION

1. As a Process Consultant being called by the new president to help him transform the university, how would you begin to work with him? What does Client-centered Helping look like here? Where would Helping be centered within the university as a Client (where would you locate the dots in the Figure 7 diagram)?
2. What initial questions should the Process Consultant ask the president? What would a Process Design begin to look like from the work done already and what would the next steps be to bring it into being?
3. As the Client is both the organization and its people, who in this case would be the Client? Just the president? The president and the board? The whole university? A subset?
4. What resources might be drawn upon as a process is designed and carried out? How might choosing those resources further center the work within the Client?

The Sixth Core Competency

HELPING: CLIENT-OWNED AND CLIENT-INSPIRED

Successful Process Consultants begin and build their practice around the impact satisfied Clients can achieve in fulfillment of their mission. The Process Consultant chooses vocational freedom to partner well with Clients and to repeatedly cultivate this impact together.

Many people connected to a Client will not view matters in this same way. Almost all people tied to a Client are employees who chose the security and perceived stability of employment established by others rather than freedom to repeatedly and creatively engage adaptive change from their sense of independence. Where the Process Consultant feels confidence as they approach adaptive change, the Client often experiences anxiety. Where the Process Consultant has learned to love their work, people connected to the Client might not love their work, or they might fear exposure and embarrassment over their work thus far. Where the Process Consultant might repeatedly experience the benefit of taking risks, the Client might be risk averse.

Yes, the non-anxiousness of the Process Consultant might be reassuring and be a reason they are retained. Yes, listening well can uncover Client anxiety or resistance and help the Process Consultant move more adroitly, but this appeal will be short-lived. Without the Client's own inspiration for and ownership over the process, the Client is highly unlikely to do the sustained work that adaptive and transformational change requires.

The Consultant's freedom and apparent calm might get them in the Client's door and get an Agreement signed. The Client's need for security just might throw the Consultant back out.

ITERATION AND EMANATION

The words *iteration* and *emanation* mean a great deal in Process Consulting. What do you know about these words? What do they mean to you? How would you use them in a sentence? Both words come into play when helping Clients grow their inspiration and ownership for their process.

Consider a calm body of water. You touch the water and ripples flow outward from the point of impact to the edges that hold it. Each time you touch it those ripples become stronger until a current can be formed and continue for a time even when you've stopped touching the surface of the water. Touching the water is *iteration*. Ripples and currents are *emanations.*

HELPING: CLIENT-OWNED AND CLIENT-INSPIRED

To build understanding of iteration and emanation, we can begin by remembering the two key Client questions that summarize the *why, who, what, when, where,* and *how* of a Client Agreement.

- *What do you need to do?*
- *What are you willing to do?*

Then we might revisit the needed and normal progression of each Client meeting while working through an adaptive process.

- Here is why we are working together—a reminder of the mission.
- That is where we were.
- Here is where we are.
- This is what we are doing now (Adaptive Conversation).
    - —What do we have here?
    - —Shall we adjust anything in our process because of what we now have?
- There is where we go next.
    - —Identify next steps between now and the next stage gate

Why, who, what, when, where, and *how* is an *iteration*. Each subsequent Client meeting when the adaptive conversation takes place is also an iteration.

When you identify the *who* of a Client Agreement, you are defining the center. These are the people who make the process happen. Each conversation beyond the people at the center meeting to advance the process is an *emanation*. Emanations go out from the center as these key players move among, communicate with, and invite others to participate in adaptive change activity.

Each time the Client revisits a process it is an *iteration*.

Each time the Client communicates about the process it is an *emanation*—whether the communication is done informally in private conversation or, publicly in a communiqué for everyone.

Each degree of emanation away from this center dilutes the strength of inspiration and ownership to follow through, especially if emanations are not reinforced over time. Each degree of emanation away from the center requires deliberately planned time to build commitment to act, just as those at the center had their time to determine whether this was what they were willing to do.

To build consistent and reinforcing iteration and emanation we can learn from two key activities found in Agile Methodology. They are (1) Customer Collaboration and (2) Responding to Change.

Customer Collaboration requires constant feedback loops that help to reinforce Client-ownership and to further confirm that what is being worked on grows from Client inspiration rather than external prescription from the consultant, or orders from on high.

Responding to Change is growing from those feedback loops and the adaptive conversations they enable, the roadmap within the Process Design can be adjusted to what is being learned and what appears to be the next step.

Iterations repeatedly invite and strengthen ownership.
Each iteration gives opportunity to set a new round of emanations.
Emanations provide opportunity to repeatedly inspire interest
in the next iteration.
And so on.
Repeated iterations and emanations build a current in the flow that moves
everyone along, almost despite themselves.
The Process Consultant cannot make anyone do anything.
The Process Consultant can help the Client make change exciting and desirable
by staying focused on a collaborative and responsive process.

HELPING: CLIENT-OWNED AND CLIENT-INSPIRED

WORKING THROUGH A SEEMING CONTRADICTION

How do we reconcile the seeming contradiction between *que sera sera* non-anxiousness with urgent and intensive forward planning? How do we do this in the face of Client anxiety and desire for assurance when none of us can guarantee adaptive and transformational results?

The Process Consultant's power is quite limited. What they can offer is a partnership of concentrated focus on what the Client has declared they are willing to do, the steps the Client outlines they will take, and the iterations and emanations along the way. One way to build this in partnership with the Client is through yet another question the Process Consultant can repeatedly ask CEOs and Executive Directors: *Do they, their board, and their key players have five years of patience?*

Change at the depth of adaptation and transformation usually takes:

- *1-2 years* to intentionally create the *awareness* of the need to change and to build the desire to change.[31] Sometimes, in crisis, this stage shortens up. Usually, however, the changes a Client is now ready to make are those they've been resisting for a year or two already. They cannot postpone the change any longer because it would be too painful.

- Consider the example of virtual meetings. A great number of people who made the transition in the COVID era did so because they lost all other options of meeting in person. Now they are saving money and time that they could have saved all along and they embrace it. Some are embracing it with the same passion with which they once abhorred it. This previously resisted change is reflected in many of the Case Studies contained in this book!

- *A year* to implement the change and for people to become comfortable in their *knowledge* of its requirements and their role (this is sometimes noted as a year of working without a net).

- *A year* to live into the change, during which the *ability* to live into

THE SIXTH CORE COMPETENCY

the new reality grows. This year becomes a baseline year upon which trend lines can be established.

- *A year* in which changes are *reinforced.* This fifth year is the comparative year, during which new trend lines are tracked.

There is a lot of resistance to the notion that it takes five years to foster needed and lasting change in an established organization. Clients are tempted to think they are the exception. They might protest that their level of experience, the force of their will, or the demands of a changing marketplace make them the exception. They too often close their minds to the care and detail it takes to implement major change and make it stick.

Go faster than five years and watch the carnage pile up. Perhaps extensive personnel turnover is needed to rescue a company. With a five-year intentionality, making those personnel change becomes the preparation exercise of years 1-2, rather than a painful necessity in years 4-5 when leaders remove painful blockages to changes they unsuccessfully tried to implement.

Plan for a shorter horizon and remove the ability to learn as you go. Perhaps leaders do know the right answer, the best solution, and the correct tools. Implementing them by throwing everyone into the deep end of a new pool, however, and the time that it takes to get in a new flow together, quickly uses up 1-2 years.

Fail to account for this five-year horizon and discover how difficult it becomes to manage contingencies and incorporate new insight. Perhaps you've lived through such a change elsewhere, but it wasn't here. It was in a different context and context is rarely if ever identical. Think through the time it took you to learn and develop new ability the previous time. Others need to same opportunity.

Can it go faster? Under unique circumstances, perhaps. However, it can also go more slowly than we prefer. Regardless of the time it takes, fast or slow, *leadership craftsmanship requires focused attention for a sustained period.* Fast or slow, there are no shortcuts for developing inspiration and ownership, for the needed reinforcing iterations and emanations. We can scarcely make it go faster, but we can sure make it go slower or fail altogether through arrogance, denial, misuse of power, and belief we are somehow exempt.

Does the Client have this length and depth of attention span to foster and implement major change? Are you, as a Process Consultant, repeatedly naming this dynamic as the Client iterates their process and then communicates in waves of emanation? If the answer is something other than yes, the Process Consultant's alarm bells should be ringing. A key signpost of Client inspiration and ownership is that they can imagine giving themselves to five years of sustained effort.

Patient and sustained attention is a leadership virtue. The Process Consultant is wise to cultivate patience and sustained attention as they help. It is good if the Process Consultant brings a certain amount of energy to their help, but this is no substitute for the Client being inspired to name what they will do and to own it so thoroughly that they will patiently attack their "it" with agile waves of gain.

Helping: Client-Owned and Client-Inspired
CASE STUDIES

1. A firm foundation

Background. Huntington Health is a midwestern hospital system that has delivered quality healthcare to more than 100,000 people for over 100 years. The hospital is a large employer and has played an important economic role in the success of the region.

Under the leadership of its president, Randy Christopher, and the steady hand of its Board of Directors, the hospital built significant financial reserves and leads its competitors in world-class cancer care, heart and vascular care, and orthopedic and sports medicine. Because of its size and scope, the hospital provides millions of dollars in philanthropic funding to many non-profit organizations in its community.

Over the past decade and in large part because of the lack of innovation in the healthcare industry, increased competition from national health care providers, and reduced funding by insurance providers, Huntington Health is experiencing increased financial pressures and demands for systemic change.

While philanthropy formed the basis of Huntington Health and the farmland on which the hospital was built resulted from a charitable gift, Huntington Health has not typically been the recipient of outside philanthropy. To help meet these changing needs, seven years ago the hospital formed a foundation, with a separate board, and tasked a group of community leaders and volunteers to build a new stream of revenue for the hospital. As a result, Jim Raskin was hired to guide the Foundation and recently completed a $15 million capital campaign to build a new hospital wing, further enhancing patient care.

Building on this success, the leadership of the Foundation, with Randy Christopher's approval, retained a Process Consultant to help them better understand the potential future impact philanthropy can have on Huntington Health and the overall healthcare of its region.

PROCESS DESIGN

Why **are we doing this?** Through the dedication and hard work of the campaign's volunteer leadership as shepherded by Jim Raskin, the recent campaign was an overwhelming success. Never in Huntington Hospital's history has this level of philanthropic support been generated from the community.

Before moving forward with any additional fundraising efforts, Jim Raskin desires to take a step back and develop a set of vision priorities, that if funded and met, could lead the Hospital Foundation into an even brighter future.

Who plays what role as we address this?
- Randy Christopher and Huntington Hospital's Board of Trustees are the final decision-makers on any future fundraising effort and realize that leadership for these efforts must come from Jim Raskin and his advancement team, and that it is essential to have the buy in from the Foundation's Board of Directors.
- The Process Consultant will facilitate an organizational discovery process to identify potential vision priorities.
- Those involved in this discovery process will be determined by Jim Raskin and will come from both internal and external audiences of Huntington Hospital including donors, key medical staff, and both boards of the hospital and foundation.
- As these vision priorities emerge, Jim Raskin seeks to further engage Randy Christopher and his board in understanding the role philanthropy can have on the future of the entire hospital system.

What criteria do we look to know that we succeeded? We will develop a set of vision priorities that, if funded, further position Huntington Health as the resource for excellent healthcare in the region. Through this process, we also seek to:
- Create a robust strategic plan that directs and inspires the work of Huntington Health's Foundation.
- Write a case for support (our story to tell) that engages the broader community and region in our transformative work.
- Deepen the network of donors and partners who capture this bold vision for the future.
- Envision a robust advancement office that supports the funding

of this vision, positioning Huntington Health as a philanthropic leader in the community.

- Position Huntington Health Foundation as an interdependent component of the overall health care system's strategic future.

When do we wish this work to be completed?
- Overall process to be completed by the end of the calendar year.

    —Providing 90 days to conduct the discovery process and uncover the vision priorities, presenting them for affirmation to the hospital and foundation board of directors.

    —An additional 90 days is given to develop and bring consensus to the Foundation's philanthropic strategic plan and road map forward, presenting them for final approval by the hospital's board of directors.

- Strategic plan and road map will further outline quarterly targets for the next fiscal year.

Where will this work take place? Given the short timeline, dispersion of Board members, and schedules of the medical professionals, work will take place at 1 Hospital Drive, via video technology. One-on-one meetings with key individuals will take place at a location of their designation.

How will we complete this work?
- The Process Consultant and Jim Raskin will develop and initiate a consensus-building process that develops a set of vision priorities by engaging leadership through facilitated in-person dialogue as well as through an online survey that gathers further feedback, insight, and imagination.

    —Up to five virtual town-hall style meetings that ask and answer important questions about the hospital's future.

    —Up to 20 individual meetings with key stakeholders.

    —One online survey that asks 4-6 questions.

- Utilizing the emerging vision priorities, the Process Consultant and Jim Raskin will co-create a robust strategic plan that directs and inspires the work of Huntington Health Foundation's Board of Directors. They will also co-create:

    —A case for support that captures these vision priorities, people's imagination, and tells the story of Huntington Health.

    —A plan that engages the broader community in this enterprise, positioning them to understand the role Huntington Health plays in the broader community, and how through their ongoing philanthropic investment this vision can be realized.

    —A relationship development plan that enhances relationships with internal stakeholders, in particular Huntington Health's executive team, to develop partnerships, create synergies, and enhance creativity.

    —Lon Swartzentruber

FOR PROCESS CONSULTANT DISCUSSION

1. What challenges might exist as hospital leadership discovers the role philanthropy can take within the overall health care system?
2. With all of the audience involved in the work of this Agreement (Randy Christopher, Jim Raskin, two boards of directors) where might there be alignment, where might they differ?
3. What questions might you ask to further flesh out Client ownership and inspiration, develop an architecture for a healthy, owned and inspired process, while also uncovering potential landmines?
4. How would the end of this process be described by those involved: A transformed foundation with a vision for the future? Incremental steps to move both systems forward? Something else?

2. A cash flow uh-oh!

Alison Moriarity put her phone down, bemused. "That's the third time this month I've been called with a scenario like this," she informed the empty air.

Alison was a Process Consultant with CFO credentials. Pat Wang, her colleague down the hall, was an expert in operations, and together they'd formed an organizational development firm five years ago with a focus on the intersection between operations and finance. Their Process Consulting approach had already gained them a reputation for listening and designing with Clients, rather than telling and prescribing.

"We've another one!" Alison announced, not bothering to knock.

Pat closed her laptop and looked up. "Tell me."

Alison scrolled through her notes. "This time it's Acme Tools. They're a manufacturer of highly machined and long-lasting carpentry tools. They put a comprehensive operating system in place six months ago to tie inventory turns, employee time, machine usage and maintenance, purchasing, and shipping together. All of this now integrates with their accounting system and KPI reports. And just like the other two Client Consulting Agreements we signed with the golf resort and the department store chain; they're suddenly running into inexplicable cash flow issues."

"Huh." Pat leaned back in her chair. "This is getting to be a trend. Do you think the same issues are in play?"

"Even if they are the same issues, telling them that their financial staff has likely begun batching invoices and deposits to accommodate the administrative demands of their new software, rather than paying attention to cash flow, isn't going to be readily understood. Company ownership and the staff responsible for this are going to need to join in the discovery, or else they'll just tweak their cash flow management and not get at the deeper issue. Their use of the new software is weakening their overall approach to problem-solving."

"How bad is it?"

Alison grimaced. "They just got a call from their bank telling them their most recent financial reports show a worsening debt-to-equity ratio that puts them out of covenant. Even though they're operating profitably, they dipped into their line of credit for nearly seven figures over the past six weeks, when they hadn't touched it for the last three years. The Board is aghast, and the CEO is angry and ashamed. He actually used those words. They want a proposal from us ASAP."

Pat snapped her laptop open again to consult her calendar. "Breakfast tomorrow morning? We can whiteboard a proposal that starts with a Process Design. I'll bring the coffee."

—Mark L. Vincent

FOR PROCESS CONSULTANT DISCUSSION

1. If you were Alison, what questions would you have asked when the potential Client called you?
2. Who is the Client in this case? Specifically, as a Process is designed, who would be playing what role? How might their ownership and inspiration make or break a successful outcome?
3. How would you outline a proposal for this Client, especially with the need for Client ownership and inspiration in mind? How would you price your service for facilitating this Consulting Agreement and why?
4. If you were in the room forming a straw figure draft of a Process Design with Alison and Pat, what answers for *why, who, what, when, where,* and *how* would emerge?

The Seventh Core Competency

HELPING: CLIENT-SPECIFIC

A Client-centered solution can only be implemented successfully when the Client owns the process and is inspired to act in a sustained and adaptive manner. A Client-owned and inspired action also takes place in the Client's specific context.

But what is meant by context? Merriam-Webster offers two descriptions in its definition:

1. Context is the parts of a discourse that surround a word or passage and can throw light on its meaning.
2. Context is the interrelated conditions in which something exists or occurs. Those conditions produce an environment or setting.

It is good to soak inside these definitions for a while. Please take a moment to read them a second time. And then, a third. Put them in your own words in writing. Then turn the paper over and say them out loud. Then say them in someone else's hearing and have a conversation about these definitions. Use them in a sentence. Tell some stories about your experiences with the specifics of context.

Returning to the definition, context is:

- Words and definitions—which weave us back to the second Core Competency of Listening Conceptually and Contextually.
- Setting and conditions—which are interrelated and should remind the Process Consultant and the Client that the solution growing out of a process will bring effect and be affected by a unique ecosystem with its own culture.

A THOUGHT EXPERIMENT

Another way to understand the importance of Client-specific solutions for the Process Consultant is to conduct a thought experiment. What if a solution offered to a Client was completely generic, without any respect for the Client's experience, expertise, uniqueness, or any adjustment to setting or timing? What if the solution were context-less, without any flexibility to Client specifics? What if there was no adaptability at all to the solution? How desirable would that solution be? How committed would the Client be to using and sustaining it? How would the role of a Process Consultant change when it comes to implementation and assistance?

Without Client specificity, a solution is merely a pre-packaged product. The Helping role of product implementation becomes that of contractor or project manager or vendor or subject matter expert. Process Consulting disappears.

Context is to process as precedent is to product. A Process Design pays attention to process. The result of this process is a product of some sort. Use of this product sets a precedent within the organization.

Said a little more artfully:

There isn't anything context free.
And there isn't anything precedent free.
Context (process) and precedent (product) flow together.
The difference is what is placed first in the equation.

HELPING: CLIENT-SPECIFIC

Subject Matter Experts tend to start with a *precedent* formed elsewhere as they work with a Client. They might tailor that solution for the Client, but precedent is what gets drawn upon for the work.

Process Consultants, because they start with process, are starting with *context* as they work with a Client. As a process reveals possibilities to pursue, the Client and Process Consultant might draw on some precedents, especially if they are part of the Client's context and fit with Client-defined objectives, but it is the process that serves as centerpiece of the experience.

We can think of this dynamic of precedent (product) and context (process) as a continuum. First, the Process Consultant (Figure 12):

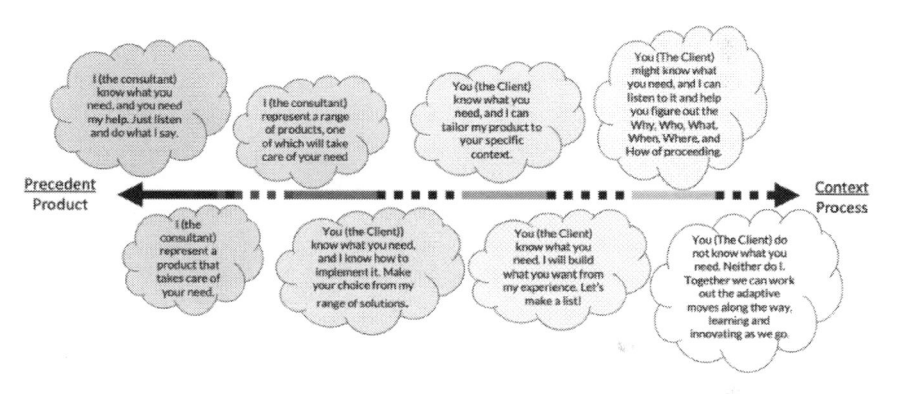

Figure 12

Now, the Client using this same continuum (Figure 13):

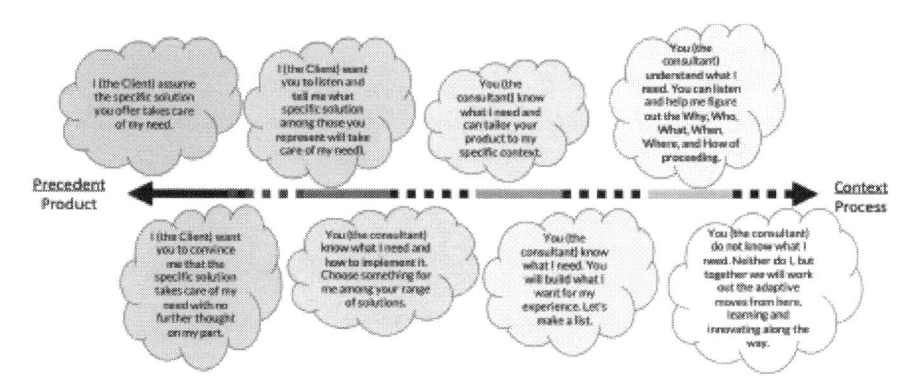

Figure 13

131

Note the movement from darker to lighter shades along the shaft of the arrows as you move through the thought clouds from left to right. Whether they are above or below the line is not of relevance here, just the left to right continuum. It moves from a precedent that produced a product for everyone on the left side toward a specific process for a specific context on the right. You might guess that the lighter-shaded the statement becomes, the purer the form of Process Consulting. Also, notice how much more Client-specific it becomes, not just because the Client has said they want it, but because the Client is listening to themselves and identifying specifics within their specific context.

It is difficult to practice Process Consulting if the consultant is oriented to the left side of the continuum. The further to the right the Process Consultant moves, the more able they are to be helpful to a Client, regardless of where a Client might be placed. From the right side of the continuum a Process Consultant is able to modulate themselves to a Client's specific perspective.

THE IMPORTANCE OF CLIENT-SPECIFIC CONTEXT

Climbing a previously unclimbed rock wall is a context specific action. Experience is helpful but the experienced climber is foolish to think what they have always done will be all they need to see them up the wall. Yes, there are other rock walls, but each is unique. A breakthrough climb will, even for an experienced climber, require specific knowledge and educated anticipation of surprises during the previously untried climb. They need to eye the climb, practice it repeatedly in their minds, and review their questions every bit as much as their answers. The untried climb is context specific.

Tools are helpful in climbing a previously unclimbed rock wall. Even in an unroped free climb, tools are in play. The climber needs a prepared body and mind, clothing appropriate to the weather, chalk powder to reduce slippage, and shoes that grip. How does the climber know what tools to bring? She or he brings their tools as a guardianship of the climb, a means to frame up and then govern their efforts.

Journeying into an unknown future does not mean a pioneer has no experience or tools. And it does not mean the pioneer thinks the context is the same every time a new path gets blazed. Similarly, as the Process Consultant works within the specifics of the context with the Client, they do so with awareness of precedents, and are prepared to use tools that assist their partnership with the Client to figure *it* out. The tools are a means for stepping stones to be revealed, for adaptive moves to be planned for and then evaluated, and to shorten the distance between needing to do something, being willing and preparing to do something about it, and then celebrating having done it.

TOOLS TO USE FOR CLIENT SPECIFICITY

A comprehensive explanation and demonstration of tools Process Consultants might bring to Client-specific contexts is beyond what this book can convey. As a starting point, however, here is a quick list of tools with a description.

1. Process Design. Process Design is the original and ongoing iteration of the scope of work with the Client, using the questions, *why, who, what, when, where,* and *how* See the opening chapter of this book for more information.

2. Framing Exercises.[32] A framing exercise sets a common definition for the problem to be addressed, and within what points of view. While a Process Design serves as a framing exercise, a Process Design can also expose a need to do further framing. For instance: an executive team stuck within a financial planning process might be thinking exclusively about financial impacts for the year ahead, consistently referring to next year's budget. Changing the frame to consider financial impacts over the next three to five years provides a new framework around the problem and a means to think differently. The Process Consultant might ask, *What changes if you give this a three to five year forecast in comparison to just the next budget year?* They might provide a related worksheet, inviting thinking about impact to top, middle and bottom line for a key decision across one, three and five years. The Process Consultant is not providing answers but is watching for and then helping to overcome blinders that limit perspective.

3. Market Research.[33] Without current and reliably constructed data, it can be hard to define a problem, let alone identify possible approaches and then decide. Polling, focus groups, database reports, and in-person interviews are just some of the ways to gather and draw upon past and current data, as well as make forecasts.

4. Triangulation.[34] This tool is a personal favorite, especially when a problem is difficult to define, or possible solutions are stubborn to uncover. In essence, triangulation looks at a problem from at least three angles to discover what they might hold in common. Sometimes this helps to better define the problem. And, often, triangulation uncovers a critical path forward.

5. Weighted Decision Making.[35] Sometimes a process reveals multiple ways forward, or several potential solutions. How to choose? One method for sorting is to add prioritized weight to decision-making criteria to distinguish between options. For instance, when hiring a contractor, the online ranking of service from previous customers might be given more weight than the actual price in deciding who receives the contract. Agreeing on the weight of decision-making factors brings greater thoroughness to documenting the process. Even more, it galvanizes perspective for decisions needing to be made as a group effort, as well as sets the stage for any needed public communication.

6. Supportive Training and Coaching. Process Consultants sometimes describe their work as a coach-ative approach to organizational development. And, Executive Coaches have been heard to say that they are bringing a consultative approach to coaching. This play on words grows from a realization that working with organizational leaders on organizational issues means that people must learn and grow for the organization to learn and grow. The reverse is true as well. Skills have to be developed or reinforced alongside the new initiatives being figured out and then deployed.

7. Evaluation tools.[36] A worthwhile Process Design provides checkpoints along the way where a process might be adjusted based upon what is being learned. Further, a Process Design expects that what is decided and then implemented by the Client will also be evaluated at an agreed upon time. Organizations that routinely practice evaluation will uncover new opportunities or problems to address, requiring new processes to design and then work through. Organizations that do not practice evaluation will reach stuck points where evaluation ultimately must be injected in a more interventionary way. In either case, evaluation tools, especially those that combine non-anxiousness with robust data collection, are friends to the Process Consultant and their Clients.

8. Executive Leadership Assessments.[37] A specific form of evaluation, that of evaluating those who bring executive leadership to an organization, is a helping tool for those specific leaders in their specific context. For the Process Consultant, the preferred tools are those that help individual leaders gain insight to themselves with their context and with their team in mind. Further, the preferred tools evaluate the organizational system alongside the individual or leadership team since they mutually influence one another. In other words, an evaluation of the governance system combines assessments of the individual Board members with the overall governance output.

BRINGING THIS TOGETHER

Helping a Client in a way that is specific to the Client and the Client's context is a key identifier of Process Consulting. Process Consultants who are highly developed toward Client specificity are better able to modulate to the Client's capacity for change. Process Consultants will want a broad array of tools to draw upon as they help to frame a scope of work, listen for what the Client identifies as needing and desiring to do, gathers data, and draws meaning from adaptive discovery.

THE SEVENTH CORE COMPETENCY

Helping: Client-Specific
CASE STUDIES

1. Getting groceries with your children

Background. Dinger's Food Stores is a family-owned company that operates four grocery stores in Ohio and Indiana with a combined revenue of just under $20 million. Earl Silver and his wife Ellen are co-owners of the company after having bought it nearly twenty years ago following the unexpected death of Ellen's father, George Dinger.

Ellen and Earl have three children: Samantha (Sam), Devin, and Earline, each in their early- to mid-thirties. Despite having grown up in and around the family business and having been employed by the business at one point or another, none of the three have shown strong interest in ownership or leadership of the business. Earl and Ellen have not wanted for force the business on their children. However, Earl has recently experienced some heart issues, and now in their late fifties, they need to explore what is best for the two of them, their family, and the business. The Silvers had two sets of friends who also owned businesses, and each of them had engaged an advisory board to help the owners sort out and process a host of interconnected family and business issues.

The Silvers secretly hoped their children would have indicated by now their interest in the business and they regret not having been more proactive with their kids. Sam and Earline live in the region, while Devin lives in Arizona. All three kids have modest careers that they seem happy with, but at a recent family gathering there was some playful joking among the three siblings about buying out their mom and dad so their parents could retire in Arizona like they have always said they would like to do.

Ellen's best friend Paige had mentioned recently that she and her husband were working with a Process Consultant on some challenges within their business. Ellen got the contact information and requested a conversation with the Process Consultant to explore options, including their interest in learning how an advisory board might help them make decisions.

PROCESS DESIGN

Why **are we doing this?** Earl and Ellen Silver want to eventually retire to northern Arizona where the dry air will help Ellen manage her severe asthma. With Ellen's father's unexpected death, the Silvers described to their best friends that they felt "forced" into ownership of the Dinger's Food Stores business for the sake of Ellen's mother, Georgette. The business has been providing a decent living for the Silvers over the past two decades. However, they did not want to force the business on any of their children and practically avoided ever seriously discussing this with them. As months had turned into years, they now realized they need to address everyone's longer-term interests and needs but do not feel they have the skills or capacity for such an important process.

Who **needs to be included in the exploration process?**
- Ellen and Earl Silver are the owners who will make decisions about their future, but they realize they do not want to move forward without intentionally including their three children.
- The Process Consultant will help the Silvers facilitate appropriate conversations with their three children, as well as Sam's husband Jim and Devin's significant other.
- The Silvers asked the Process Consultant to convene a small group of trusted friends, including those who owned businesses, to help them outline the components.

THE SEVENTH CORE COMPETENCY

What are our desired outcomes
- The Silvers desire several primary outcomes from this process:

  –That their children have the opportunity to participate fully and gain a deeper understanding of the business and related decisions the family will need to make about the future, including helping these young adult children determine how each will gain clarity for their own future vis-à-vis the family business.

  –That the Silver family take the necessary time to discern options for the future of the business, including:
  - One or more of the children taking leadership and/or ownership roles.
  - Selling to a competitor or other outside buyer and managing a family foundation with the proceeds from the sale of the business.
  - Developing an Employee Stock Ownership Plan (ESOP).
  - Other options that the Silvers may not yet be considering or some combination of options.

  –That the Silver family agree on a path forward in which each member of the family has had the opportunity to share meaningfully in making decisions that will impact the whole family.

- Several additional possible outcomes include:

  –Deciding whether to add an Advisory Board; and if deciding to add such a Board, to decide what role the Process Consultant will play in helping the Silvers design, recruit for, and operate an Advisory Board.

  –Assessing whether the business has employees who can be groomed to replace Earl's president role, and Ellen's part-time vital role in human resources; or whether any of the Silver children have interest and aptitude for their parents' roles; or whether the business needs to recruit one or more people externally.

When do we wish for this work to be completed?
- Timing is currently important but not yet urgent. Developing an overall timeline and likely sequence of events spanning one to two years or more needs to happen within the next one to three months in light of Earl's recent heart issues.
- Scheduling one or more family meetings—perhaps offsite in a retreat or resort setting—will best be scheduled in the next six months.
- Scheduling and inviting the Silver's small group of friends to help them discern direction can happen as soon as possible since such a meeting could help the Silvers with other planning and considerations.
- Additional meetings will be scheduled as needed depending on the outcome of the above events.

Where will this work take place?
- Meetings between Ellen and Earl Silver and the Process Consultant will happen at the Dinger's flagship store in western Ohio.
- Meetings between Ellen and Earl and their close friends can happen at the Silver residence on their screened-in deck.
- Meetings of the Silver family that includes children and significant others can take place at their cabin on Lake Michigan or other resort setting.

How will we complete this work?
- The Process Consultant will propose an overall timeline with process components to test with the Silvers for a first phase. The timeline will be adjusted as needed to assure the confidence of the

Silvers that their context is being fully considered and their needs are being completely addressed.

- The Silvers will reach out to their children to introduce the Process Consultant, after which the whole Silver family and the Process Consultant will get one or more dates on their calendars for the family off-site conversations.

- The Silvers will provide contact information for the Process Consultant to invite the Silver's friends to a four-hour gathering that begins with a catered meal. The Silvers will decide if an additional meeting will be helpful.

- The Process Consultant will steward the growing list of ideas, concerns, questions, and learnings and meet monthly with Ellen and Earl to adjust the timeline to address any surprises or mutually agreed changes, considering the complex set of factors between the needs of the family and the realities of the business.

- After the Silver family members have all declared their interests, the Process Consultant will propose a second phase of the process to address next steps toward ongoing resolution of the desired outcomes stated above.

—Philip C. Bergey

FOR PROCESS CONSULTANT DISCUSSION

1. As you consider the complexity of this case study, how would you help the Silvers uncover the many facets of the family and business interests and needs? How would you help the Silvers balance and organize the many—and sometimes competing—interests and needs? What is specific and unique about this family and their business that might not be duplicated elsewhere?

2. What strategy would you use to price your services for this case study? What are the pros and cons of using several phases? How might phasing the work address the known and emerging specifics of this Client?
3. What are the opportunities and limitations of a Process Consultant in such a complex context? Which of these would energize you and which would cause you considerable concern?
4. How would you determine if and when to collaborate with additional professional services to address specific and related needs like those offered by a family systems counselor, an attorney, an estate planner, or others? What other tools or resources might come into play here?

2. Growing operational maturity levels

Background. Advanced Operations has been around for five years, and as with most startups, they adapted their product line as they discovered what services were most cost-effective and what the market need was.

Advanced Operations serves its customers in a variety of ways through various operational third-party support resources. Their services allow customer teams to expand and scale their organizations while not having to take on the full overhead of new employees.

Teams are starting to expand at the company and excitement is building as they see the impact they are making not only for their customers but also in the community through their philanthropic efforts. The core focus of the organization is to help people—other organizations and those around them.

As a bunch of incredibly capable people, the team embraces pretty much any type of need their customers throw at them. Everyone says, "Yes! We can do that!" High-fives are celebrated when new business is landed, and companies come on board to support their efforts and the new business is handed off from sales to the operations team.

Post-handoff, questions quickly appear as to *how* they will actually do these things because they don't fit in any set offering structure or process. Stressful conversations and extra planning and coordination happen constantly to make sure what was promised to the customer can be met. Questions at the leadership level are asked about profitability and employee care and what was celebrated earlier becomes intensively high-pressure at the operational level. The joy of helping people diminishes as employees start to feel overwhelmed and unsure of their roles.

A flag is waved for the leadership team to re-evaluate their offerings and what will not only support their customers best but also build a positive environment for their employees.

PROCESS DESIGN

Why **is change needed?** As the company grew, it became less clear what services they specifically offered as each customer turned into a customized package. This brought a lot of questions and uncertainty with the team as there wasn't clear direction on how to support each customer as they came on board—customized processes, workflows, and resources were needed for each customer. Their goal as an organization was to grow and expand into new regions and industries, but they knew that the current process and product/service scope limited their scalability. Scaling without losing the ability to be customer specific is a conundrum requiring a solution that can no longer wait.

Who **is playing what role in the process?**
- **The CEO and Executive Team** set the stage for the company goals, vision, and ensure their team has the resources they need to move forward. They are the ultimate decision-makers for changes to offerings and movement in the company.

- **Three teams need to be part of shaping and implementing the solution. A cross-functional task force will be pulled together from among them.**

–**The Operations Team** provides services and support for customers. There are team members specifically skilled in certain areas to support customers. They have flexed to find roles for everything that is being sent their way, but their teams are becoming disjointed with little predictability and cross-training between team members.

–**The Sales Team** is proactively looking for new customers to support and has been selling with the mentality of "Yes! We can do that!" without specific boundaries around what specific services to offer or what the team is capable of handling.

–**The Marketing Team** is focused on finding specific industries as leads, with little qualifying details. Their focus and budget are very broad and could be optimized more fully to support the organization.

What are the desired outcomes?

- A new offering breakout needs to be identified and focused on the core strengths of the Operations Team. This breakout needs to include:

    –A detailed description of company offerings.

    –Pricing for offerings with flexible discount opportunities for the sales team to work within.

    –Examples of use cases for each offering element.

    –Examples of current customers (testimonials) for each offering element.

    –Sales pitch examples and phrasing for the sales and marketing teams with which to work.

    –Workflow handoff steps for each offering.

- Onboarding Standard Operating Procedures (SOPs) for each offering, breaking out the specific areas of support, team member workflow, and the technology and resources needed.

- New collateral and budget tied to these offerings that will guide marketing and sales efforts.
- Updates to the website to explain the new offerings.
- A communication plan for the organization to train everyone on the new offerings so each team is clear on the approach and offering.
- A strategic framework and playbook for current customers that do not fit in the new offering structure and a communication approach for any changes.

***When* is the desired timeframe to finish this work?** The task force will have five months to work through this analysis and create a schedule for desired implementations, which need to be in place within the first quarter of the next budget year.

***Where* is the work being conducted (geography and/or domain)?** With a fully remote team, all strategy sessions and meetings will take place virtually through a video conference call. The executive team will meet in person together for a final review of decisions and organizational changes.

***How* will the work happen?**
- A Process Consultant has been brought in to provide facilitative support for the task force. They will identify a roadmap to help them get to their desired outcome while keeping an open and honest outlook on each of the different team roles and responsibilities.
- In the first month, three Discovery calls will be facilitated by the Process Consultant with all key stakeholders involved. Each call will focus on the three business units impacted by the challenge at hand, seeking a unified workflow. Questions will be asked to explore their challenges, strengths, and concerns.
- The Process Consultant will review the notes from the discovery

calls and express observations and further areas for the team to discuss and dive into together in an additional joint call with all key stakeholders at the start of the second month.

- The Task Force team will take the input from the teams and work together through an off-site retreat in October with company executives to create a new structure and workflow that will better support their employees and customers.
- The Process Consultant will help coordinate the training and support materials for what has been agreed upon during the third and fourth months.

—Jennifer Miller

FOR PROCESS CONSULTANT DISCUSSION

1. This case is particularly complex as a Process Consultant brings a Client-specific approach to a Client seeking to reduce customer complexity so that it can grow its business. How is this dynamic being balanced here? Or is it?
2. Helping with a Client-specific approach means drawing out the context and complexities of a Client's situation, bringing to light *their* uniqueness and *their* needs. It means taking them on a path of exploration to discover how unique they are so they can leverage that as a strength for growth. While tensions between sales and operations are frequently experienced in organizational life, what can be noted as specific to this Client and how might that be harnessed for a successful outcome?
3. What complexities does each team face and how will that show up in a Task Force conversation? What facilitative techniques can bring together all of these specifics (customer needs, product offerings, company teams) to form a specific solution set that helps Advanced

THE SEVENTH CORE COMPETENCY

Operations scale without losing their ability to work with customer-specific needs?

4. It is a journey from the demand of having a company team's specific needs noticed, to that same team appreciating and caring about the specific needs of other teams. How will the value of each team's work be elevated and anxieties decreased within this process?

The Eighth Core Competency

HELPING: CLIENT SUCCESS

The words Customer or Client are often used interchangeably. They are not the same. Process Consultants prefer the word "Client" because mutuality is at the center of the Process Consultant and Client relationship, whereas "customer" seeks a transaction at the relational center. Process Consultants make a choice for the mutuality of Listening, Helping, and Learning at the core rather than the cold measure of transaction size, upselling potential, or anticipated revenue.

Having settled on the specific choice within the discipline of Process Consulting to use the word Client—referring to the organization and the people (together and as individuals)—we can then consider what is meant by the Client's *success*.

The phrase "Client Success" gets used interchangeably with Client Service or Support, Client Satisfaction, and Client Experience. These terms tend to be used as loose renditions of the same thing, but there are subtle differences. For Process Consulting, Client Success is the sum of Client Experience, Client Service and Client Satisfaction.

THE EIGHTH CORE COMPETENCY

Here are more precise definitions of each so that we can build a comprehensive definition:

- Client Satisfaction: A Client-reported evaluation of Client Experience and Client Service combined, one that often overflows into a Client testimonial and referral.
- Client Experience: The Client's perception of their individual and cumulative interactions with a Process Consultant and the ecosystem/platform of which the Process Consultant is a part.
- Client Service/Support: The individual and cumulative interactions of the Process Consultant and their ecosystem/platform with their Client undergirding the possibility of a long-term and trusting relationship.
- Client Success: Achieving Client-specific outcomes which the Client reports they achieved.

A diagram of Client Success might look like this (Figure 14).

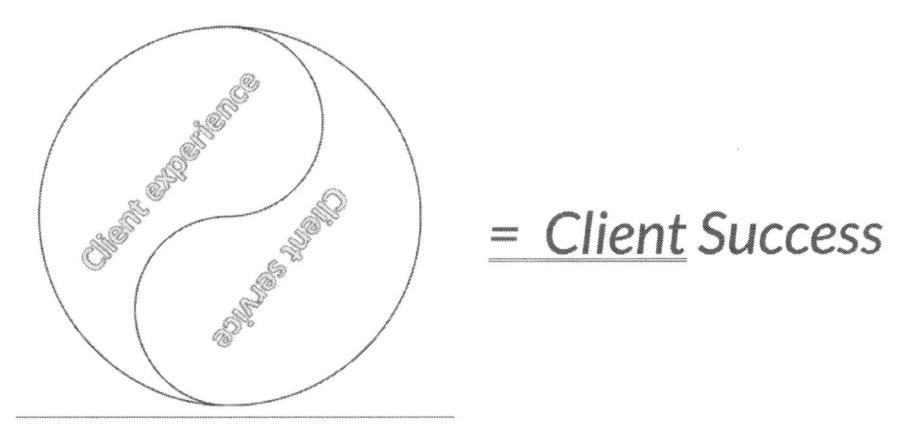

(Client experience + Client service) **CLIENT SATISFACTION** = *Client Success*

Figure 14

HELPING: CLIENT SUCCESS

In the diagram, Client Experience and Client Service are placed together in a unified whole as overlapping but distinctly different items.

Client Experience is *what the Client reports* they experience:

- "Amy is a great facilitator. She got us all got involved."
- "They seemed distracted at our last meeting, as if they wished to be elsewhere."

Client Service is *what the Process Consultant offers* in support of the Client experience:

- "Capturing Client-defined and Client-owned objectives is central to a Process Design."
- "I intend to be fully present when I facilitate a working group."

Client Satisfaction is the Client-reported aggregate of their experiences with and the services of Process Consultation. We might think of Client Experience and Client Service as what is happening in the present, while Client Satisfaction is their sum brought together as the result which is reported after the fact.

Together, Client Experience, Service, and Satisfaction are the elements that combined into Client Success.

Business and academic literature on Client Success is extensive, Search for the term "customer success loop" in a browser and then click on images. You will be awash in multitudinous examples of companies trying to describe and map how Client Success touches every aspect of their business from pre-sales marketing activity to customer referrals. Here is one such generic tool (Figure 15).

THE EIGHTH CORE COMPETENCY

Figure 15

Process Consultants need to take Client Success seriously. Keenly tracking against the Client's definition of success is a means by which a Process Consultant continues listening to the Client and remains Client-centered.

iScoop identifies four pillars commonly expressed in the literature about Client Success.[38]

1. Purposeful leadership
2. Compelling brand values
3. Employee engagement
4. Customer connectedness

Translating these four pillars into the Core Competency of Client Success, we can identify the following (please note that we change the names of the pillars slightly):

Purposeful facilitative leadership: Process Design that is designed, managed, and modified as needed with the Client.

Compelling brand values: what inspires the Client's decision to choose and stay with the Process Consultant, and with the process. For example:

- Listening—the Process Consultant's posture
- Helping—the Process Consultant's partnership
- Learning—the Process Consultant's service

Ecosystem engagement: Consistent professional and brand behaviors across the ecosystem when a Client interacts with the Process Consultant's colleagues and administrative platform. These interactions strengthen the Client relationship rather than dilute or harm it.

Client connectedness: Clients will talk with each other, either formally or informally. A consistency of Client Success reinforces brand strength and the continued opportunity to help current and future Clients live into their vibrant future again and then again.

It is appropriate for the Process Consultant to evaluate their Helping performance in each of these four pillars. What might be done next to build and strengthen them to further Client Success?

Helping: Client Success
CASE STUDIES

1. Peacemaking expansion

Background. Six years ago, Jackie Rosen, a 12-year-old middle school student, was killed in an after-school fight between two other students. His mother and uncle have channeled grief into establishing a nonprofit, Jackie's Club, that teaches kids how to manage their emotions and resolve conflict in nonviolent ways.

With the guidance of psychologists and social workers, they developed a classroom module. Once this process was complete, Barbara and Frank Rosen engaged a Process Consultant, who helped facilitate a rollout to Philadelphia's 16 public middle schools. At her recommendation, they commissioned a longitudinal study to gather data on how engaged students and teachers are with the program. Early results are overwhelmingly positive, with before and after surveys of students indicating an 88% increase in their ability to see conflict from different points of view.

After hearing from the Rosens that their volunteer-driven organization was often bogged down by day-to-day tasks, the Process Consultant recommended adding virtual administrative support of ten hours/month. She referred them to a company that provides this assistance specifically for non-profits. As a result, Jackie's Club can more efficiently answer routine questions from school staff and acknowledge donors in a timely fashion.

The Process Consultant also encouraged Jackie's Club leadership to subscribe to an eNewsletter, where curated content and client milestones and success stories are shared.

Jackie's Club, now incorporated as a 501(c)(3) charitable organization by its volunteer Board of Directors, established their mission as follows: *By teaching kids to articulate their emotions and to perceive and respect differing viewpoints, we will help build a new generation of peacemakers.* Barbara and Frank now wish to expand Jackie's Club beyond their home city and envision adding chapters in ten major U.S. cities. Based on their previous success with their Process Consultant (positive service + experience + satisfaction), they asked her to develop and facilitate the steps for a multistate expansion.

Why **are we doing this?** The articles of incorporation for Jackie's Club state that the organization will be a resource for urban youth across the U.S. While Jackie's Club's parent organization will supply the training module, and be responsible for its evolution over time, the primary mechanism for program delivery will lie within the city chapters.

We will be doing this work to ensure Jackie's Club has an effective strategic plan that will enable it to successfully expand its footprint city by city until it reaches its designated geographic expansion goal. This will require a plan and process to work with volunteers in each city to create the new chapters and to recruit the volunteers and funding resources to enable a successful program rollout.

Multistate awareness of Jackie's Club, as well as leveraging local resources in support of the additional city chapters, will be necessary to reach success. Brand awareness and alignment city to city will further strengthen the message and the mission.

All chapters will also need guidance, education, and information on best practices for nonprofit organizations to become fully functional and effective. Building strong leadership and securing the resources to build capacity will also be critical to fulfilling the plan.

Who plays what roles in this process?

- Jackie's Club's Board of Directors is ultimately responsible for addressing its mission and vision. The Board will be responsible for adopting the road map and aligning resources for success.

- The Process Consultant will facilitate discussions among the Board and key organization stakeholders, helping them design a road map with specific objectives and a sequence of action steps enabling them to effectively expand capacity of the primary organization, while expanding the footprint of the organization to other U.S. cities.

- The Board will assume oversight and some implementation responsibilities through the standing committees of the organization. Their efforts will align with the objectives outlined in the road map.

- Professional assistance will be required, including an executive, program development, and project management support. Professional assistance will be specifically identified in the road map with roles and responsibilities well defined. Jackie's Club plans to support each new chapter with virtual administrative support from the same company they now use, ensuring operations are effective and consistent from chapter to chapter.

- A nonprofit attorney will provide needed resources in creating chapter documents, specifically an agreement between the chapter and the parent organization to ensure that chapters operate in compliance with the parent group.
- Bookkeeping and accounting will be outsourced resources.

***What* criteria will we look for to know that we succeeded?**
- A presence for Jackie's Club in ten additional cities is achieved.
- Engagement of participating teachers and youth across the expanded program continues to be measured at levels comparable to those in the pilot program.
- New city chapters are functioning effectively from an operational standpoint.
- Adequate resources are available and sustainable annual revenue met.
- The brand is protected and expanded.
- A vibrant multistate community has been created, supporting a more empowered and peaceful generation.
- All chapters operate in accordance with the "Standards of Excellence" guidelines for nonprofits.

***When*, *where*, and *how* will this work be accomplished?**
- The work will be accomplished through planning sessions with leadership and key stakeholders, facilitated by the Process Consultant, and held at the Client's Philadelphia headquarters.
- The Board and strategic planning committee will continue to meet regularly to assess progress and make necessary modifications.

- The Client realizes that expanding to ten additional U.S. cities will take some time, and the national organization will need to grow its own infrastructure to support the increasing number of state organizations. The Client, the Board, and Process Consultant have agreed to a five-year time frame.
- The road map will be built in one-year strategic increments to ensure necessary benchmarks for each city chapter and the parent organization are set and met along the way.
- The road map will identify steps by quarter and by year for the period of five fiscal years.
- The Board and strategic planning committee will meet regularly to assess progress against the road map and make necessary modifications.
- The Process Consultant will participate in the quarterly evaluation of the road map, with reports to be shared with leadership.

—Vicki Burkhart

FOR PROCESS CONSULTANT DISCUSSION

1. Which of the criteria for success listed above are within the Process Consultant's control and which ones are dependent on the Board/leadership/volunteer ecosystem?
2. What ingredients within this process would constitute high success/high satisfaction? What would constitute high success/low satisfaction and low success/high satisfaction?
3. What steps has this Process Consultant taken to increase her agency in ensuring that high satisfaction and high success will both be achieved?
4. By listening to this Client's challenges and guiding them to meet their initial objective, this Process Consultant has already established

herself as a trusted partner/advisor. Regular evaluation of the expansion road map against its benchmarks, and subsequent collaborative fine tuning, will ensure this relationship remains vibrant and the Client's objectives remain in sight. Ongoing engagement with the Process Consultant's ecosystem also points to a successful and evolving long-term relationship. Do you agree with this description? Why or why not?

2. Keep on trucking

Dean Morelli stifled a sigh as he rejoined his wife at the dinner table. She raised an eyebrow.

"Something wrong? Who was that on the phone?"

Dean picked up his fork and waved it absently while he spoke. "Remember how we helped Freight Concern last year with their succession plan? I think they were pretty happy about it. They ended up with a modified ESOP. We introduced them to a business valuator, an estate planner, a charitable foundation to help them manage some charitable giving that reduced their tax liability—they really tapped all our networks! The founding family retained majority control and Jim Croat, the founder, was able to retire and turn the reins over to his daughter Marybelle."

Corinne Morelli nodded. "Oh, I remember them. They were your largest customer last year, so I got familiar with the name during all the time I spent on bookkeeping. I remember they took up a lot of *your* time, too."

Dean's fork came to rest on the table with a gentle tap. "Well, that was Marybelle on the phone. It isn't going well at the moment. Her father doesn't know what to do with himself. He keeps wandering in about the time mail is delivered and wants to actually sort through all of the envelopes. He's been hanging out behind the dispatcher's area a couple of hours each day, watching everything, listening in on conversations, making comments. Marybelle said that he acts like he still owns the place. Their lead logistics person and two dispatchers quit over his meddling and Marybelle's failure to deal with it quickly. That level of talent has been extremely hard to replace because Freight Concern handles specialty freight over long distances. Not just any trucking company does that. The new receptionist feels intimidated by him and is threatening to leave, too. I think that was the sum of what she listed. It's a lot, and it's coming at her fast."

"Eek." Corinne speared a bite of salad, then paused. "Did you set up an appointment with her?"

"Yep, but not for two weeks. Marybelle wants to confront her dad this weekend and enlisted her mom and brother to assist. She wants to transform this into something where her dad's energy can be used for mentoring within the industry. She doesn't want to just treat this as 'Stop bothering us!' or trying to keep an old man distracted. She wants to help him point his energy to something productive and meaningful. She's even going to pay for him to meet with a business coach."

"Good for her!"

Dean smiled in agreement and finally turned his attention to his half-eaten meal. "I'm meeting with Marybelle *after* all this is set up. She wants me to help her design a tailored talent recruitment, development, and retention program for Freight Concern. She figures they have to start growing their own talent and not rely so much on recruiting from elsewhere."

Corinne reached for another slice of bread. "Sounds like Marybelle is a courageous person."

"She's a lot like her father," Dean agreed through a mouthful of chicken. "They both face into hard situations with bravery. Hopefully they come through this one also."

—Mark L. Vincent

THE EIGHTH CORE COMPETENCY

FOR PROCESS CONSULTANT DISCUSSION

1. What do you suspect are the reasons that Marybelle would reach out to Dean Morelli and confide in him at this level?
2. It appears that Dean has sold a new Client Agreement without selling anything. Why do you think this is?
3. What issues are in play here for Marybelle and Freight Concern? Are they enmeshed or separated? Are they being addressed in a proper order and a healthy manner? Would you take this on if you were Dean? Why or why not?
4. Drawing from Process Consulting, if you were Dean, how would you set up a Client Consulting Agreement for this process? How would you begin crafting *why, who, what, when, where,* and *how*?

LEARNING

The Ninth Core Competency

LEARNING IN PARTNERSHIP

A full use of the Listening Core Competencies by a Process Consultant invites the Client to listen to themselves just as fully.

A full use of Helping Core Competencies by the Process Consultant brings tools, aids, lenses, frameworks, facilitation, and perhaps subject matter expertise. The Helping Core Competencies assist the Client as they move from listening for what needs to be done to declaring and then acting upon what they are willing to do.

A full use of Learning Core Competencies brings opportunity for the Process Consultant to ask the Client, *What do we have here?* This specific question helps:

- Data gives shape to insight.
- Curated information assists the possibility of creating something new.
- Organizational learning set the stage for becoming a learning organization.
- Organizational knowledge become lasting organizational wisdom.

THE NINTH CORE COMPETENCY

Turning to the Core Competencies tied to Learning, it is important to recognize that Process Consultants have frequent occasion to learn. They regularly get to embrace the benefits that come from going after an opportunity. Ideally a Client is also highly developed, growing, and eager to pursue an opportunity. Often, however, a Client is under-developed, immature, and has layers of unconscious and conscious resistance against pursuit of opportunity. Client resistance often combines with a deeper motivation to avoid anything perceived as painful. This resistance to opportunity and avoidance of pain may be embedded in an institutional structure or systems, in an organizational culture, in people wielding informal or formal power, and often in combination.

Insightful leaders of Client organizations know this is often the case and will choose to embrace a process that can help their organization confront resistance and avoidance so that they can build and grow. Unawakened leaders of Client organizations, by contrast, will consciously or unconsciously enforce their normal and undermine a process, even if they verbally and enthusiastically support it.

Insightful Process Consultants discover who these leaders are—those leading informally as well as formally—so that they can and will consciously assist this journey. The Process Consultant practicing a learning partnership discovers how these leaders learn. They work with these leaders to uncover what needs to be learned and the stepping stones along the way. They learn alongside the Client as they travel with them.

If the Process Consultant cannot identify who these leaders are and yet accepts the Client engagement anyway, they will find they have become mercenary and that no-one is learning what the Client had hoped to learn. The engagement might pay but completing any process and/or implementing its results will likely fail.

The iterative questions *why, who, what, when, where,* and *how,* and the Process Design that results, therefore, are critical to creating the map of identifying and accepting the current normal while embracing the process toward something more ideal or desired. *Who,* in particular, is an essential iterative question to answer thoroughly. Counselors and those who coach are taught to ask *What else?* several times until their Client has emptied their well of information and can think of nothing else. Process Consultants do well to ask, *Who else?* as well as *Who ARE they?* in the same way, until there is greater assurance that everyone who can either build or derail has been identified. It also helps to ensure that all who are involved have opportunity to learn and put that learning to use.

The learning partnership between the Process Consultant and the Client is introduced in the above section.

The chart (Figure 16) renders it more thoroughly:

The Client	The Process Consultant	Co-learning (Learning in Partnership)
Identifies the need to address	Asks iterative questions and curates thorough responses	Presenting and underlying issues
Articulates the willingness to proceed with a specific Process	Assists the framing of the issue(s) and guides the Process Design	Where motivation lies for strategic action(s), with what resources and toward what end
Embraces the Process	Facilitates and focuses the Process	Possibilities revealed through the Process
Asks and answers the question "what do we have here?"	Helps to adjust the Process Design to any revealed adaptive moves	Discoveries and new possibilities that might become Processes of their own
Learns	Learns	Data--> Information--> Knowledge--> Expertise--> Wisdom
Adapts to what is learned and re-engages the Process	Guides and then facilitates any adaptive moves within the Process.	Where motivation lies for adaptive moves, with what resources and toward what end
Transforms	Supports and helps to ground transformation	What decision(s) and actions to introduce/discuss/decide/implement/evaluate/adjust
Identifies new opportunities to address	Supports Client ability to begin engaging iterative questions on their own, and ready to assist again if called upon	Functioning as a **learning organization** and converting knowledge to organizational wisdom

Figure 16

Client aspects of the learning partnership are of particular importance. If they are not embraced, and in sequence, the possibility of ongoing transformation diminishes and/or disappears. On the other side of this learning partnership, the Process Consultant can harm/limit the process if they are not open to learning. By remaining open to learning, the Process Consultant is better able to guide the framing and resulting catalysis.

The Client is rightfully the more powerful partner in this Learning Partnership. It comes naturally because the objectives of the Process are Client-defined and Client-owned rather than focused on the Process Consultant. The Process Consultant is privileged to be present and to be awed by Client transformation, to learn, and thereby perhaps be further transformed also.

LEARNING TOGETHER

What are the purposeful ends of this learning partnership? Yes, there is a *why* question answered by the Client as a process is designed. That *why* gets at the Client's "it" in a robust way if the Process Consultant listens comprehensively and conceptually and articulates it back so well that the Client says *You said it even better than we did!* But the Process Consultant does their work out of an even deeper, underlying, foundational, and grounded *why* if they want Listening, Helping, and Learning to lead toward Client, and their own, transformation. The Process Consultant needs to know their own *why*.

In determining the underlying architecture of ongoing transformation, we work backwards from what a full maturity looks like to uncover the developmental layers. We do this hoping we can recognize what might come next for people or systems that intend to transform further still.

There are a number of psychological, social, and religious approaches to development. They range from Maslow's hierarchy of needs to the practices of spiritual formation, to tai chi, to cultivated mindfulness, to Clare Graves' work on spiral dynamics, and even the ongoing academic study of the organizational life cycle. None of these systems are perfect and can rightfully be critiqued, adjusted, and built upon. They provide maps, common frames of reference we can compare, contrast, and keep refining in our ongoing process of learning in partnership.

As the domain of Process Consulting combines both personal and organizational development, the Process Consultant is helped by being able to identify developmental stages of the people and systems within themselves as well as within their Client. They do not do this to judge anyone, but to appropriately frame issues and facilitate processes so everyone can learn and grow.

Two of the more comprehensive developmental models upon which a Process Consultant might draw are Kohlberg's six stages of moral development[39] and Kegan's five orders of ego-development,[40] both of which have deep roots in the larger and historical Bildung movement from Northern Europe.[41] There are newer and more refined models, which we will see as we further describe the Learning competencies of Process Consulting, but these constructs form a base upon which many of them built or are building.

Consideration of personal and systemic development goes mind-bendingly deep very quickly as one mines the related psychological, theological, and/or philosophical works. Most time-pressured organizational leaders, especially those in their first or second turns of executive leadership development[42] will find it impossible or will be unwilling to delve this deeply. The Kohlberg model is concise, readily grasped, and can live at the intersection of both personal and organizational development — which, again, is the domain of the Process Consultant. To more quickly grasp Kohlberg's work and its relationship to Process Consulting, substitute the word "organization" for "person" and the word "organizational" for "social" in Kohlberg's chart (Fig. 17), below (note: VOP in Stage One is an acronym for *value-oriented prioritization*).

Stage	View of Persons	Social Perspective Level
6	Sees the extent to which human fallibility and frailty are impacted by communication	Mutual respect as a universal principle
5	Recognizes that contracts create norms and can increase mutual wellbeing	Contractual perspective
4	Able to grasp abstract systems of norms	Social systems perspective
3	Recognizes good and bad intentions	Social relationships perspective
2	Sees that others a) have goals and preferences, b) either conform to or deviate from norms	Instrumental egoism
1	No VOP: only self & norm are recognized	Blind egoism

Figure 17

The Process Consultant, to be an effective learning partner with a Client, must continue their own development as a person in order to bring the possibility of respect for the Client's process. If the Process Consultant continues to grow themselves, they can learn with the Client as they expand upward and outward into the rare and enduring Stage 6 organization, led by exceptional people growing into their own Stage 6 leadership.

The Process Consultant's deeper *why* is grounded in a self-transforming interconnectedness, a capacity to see what is broken in systems, and then to guide a process toward systemic healing or rebuilding so that there is a heritage and legacy of flourishing, not just for themselves but for their Clients. If the Process Consultant cannot draw from their deep *why*, they will have difficulty in listening for the Client's *why*, helping the Client connect to and grow its *why*, and then to participate in co-learning as both become more deeply grounded and transformed with the flourishing of the world in mind.

Learning in Partnership
CASE STUDIES

1. Gotham Crisis Center is stumped

Background: Gotham City Crisis Center is a large historic provider of social services located in a US major metropolitan area. They began as a drug rehab center 45 years ago and recently experienced a lot of growth including mergers with other nonprofits. Their current offerings include a women's shelter, homeless outreach, drug rehabilitation programs, addiction counseling, and training in personal finance.

The mission is focused on providing for the practical needs of people experiencing homelessness, those living in poverty, and the working poor. Marijuana has recently been legalized in their state, which is causing a lot of problems in delivering their programs. The organization has 220 paid staff in eight buildings located throughout the city. In general, there is a lack of trust in management among the staff. The organization provides a plethora of services, and the staff is spread thin. They have a few government contracts but do not rely solely on state or municipal grants. A development department raises most of its funding from individuals, churches, and local foundations.

Gotham Crisis Center has experienced recent difficulties. They were cited by the city for a food handling violation. Neighboring businesses at several of their locations pushed for the organization to relocate to a different part of the city. They also have difficulty recruiting people to work in front line positions, and consequently, more supervisory issues.

Gotham City Crisis Center is asking for an external Process Consultant to provide direction and facilitation for a set of strategic planning meetings.

PROCESS DESIGN

Why are we doing this? Given the wide array of services they provide, the executive team feels stumped about how to move forward. They want to continue to grow impact, yet they do not want to undergo any more mergers and they do not want to launch any new programs. The executive team and Process Consultant will have to "learn their way forward" together.

The organization is experiencing change fatigue. Over the last few years, the mergers and creation of new programs and building of new facilities left the staff exhausted.

The lack of trust among the staff toward leadership is the driving force for bringing in an external process consultant. The CEO is afraid that the staff might reject any "fresh vision" or "silver bullets" being handed down by the executive team. She wishes staff to feel heard in the strategic planning process.

Who **plays what roles as we address this?**
- Strategic planning will be done by 16 persons.
    - —the existing executive team. They will invite some younger middle managers to the planning meetings for the dual purpose of:
      seeking their insights, and
      developing them as future members of the executive team.
- The Process Consultant co-designed the planning process with the

executive team. The executive team wants to be more transparent with their staff than they have in the past.

- The CEO desires to be a participant in the planning process rather than the one leading it. She wants to be free to share her opinions as an equal participant.
- The Vice President of strategic planning will be one of the key players. He will monitor ongoing planning after the new strategy is rolled out.
- All 220 paid staff will have opportunity for input into this planning process in order to increase the amount of buy-in the staff will have when the new strategic plan is announced.

What criteria will we specify to know that we succeeded?
- An actionable strategic plan approved by the board will be developed.
- This plan will provide for increased impact without hiring new staff or expanding into new areas of service.
- There will be a tool to track their progress over the next three years.
- They intend for a moderately high level of buy-in from the staff.

When do we wish this work to be completed? The CEO wants planning sessions to start in July and wrap up by November. They want to be ready to implement the new plan with a three-year time frame beginning in January. They want to start the new year with a new strategy.

Where will this work take place? The planning meetings with the executive team will take place in their large meeting room. Focus group interviews with paid staff will be held at several of their facilities, which are spread across the metropolitan area.

THE NINTH CORE COMPETENCY

How **will we complete this work?**

- The Process Consultant will conduct all the focus group sessions for up to 200 paid staff and generate the questions to solicit opinions. The resulting data will be fed back to all staff unedited.
- The planning team will conduct a rigorous environmental scan of factors influencing their work, such as the local economy, lack of affordable housing, drug use patterns, municipal funding, and how the face of homelessness is changing. The team will select the most relevant areas and divide into small groups to gather the data. Each group will create a report for the planning team.
- The Process Consultant will facilitate a two-day retreat to process the interview data and results of the environmental scan, then lead the planning team to write a draft strategy.
- The CEO will seek comments from the board regarding the draft strategy. The planning team will email the draft strategy to all paid staff for comments and criticism.
- The Process Consultant will facilitate a one-day meeting to distill useful insights from the comments and for the team to write the final strategy document.
- The CEO will seek formal approval from the board for the new strategy.
- The CEO will roll out the new strategy to the staff in an appropriate manner.
- The VP of strategic planning will oversee more detailed planning at department and program levels going forward.
- The Process Consultant will lead the first 90-day strategic review with the executive team. The CEO will lead the strategic reviews from that point on.

—Jim Galvin

LEARNING IN PARTNERSHIP

FOR PROCESS CONSULTANT DISCUSSION

1. Why would an organization with a Vice President of strategic planning want to bring in an external Process Consultant to facilitate strategic planning?
2. Why would so many paid staff distrust organizational leadership? How can the trust level be rebuilt through or alongside of the strategic planning process?
3. What is the attitude of the organization and its leaders toward learning and how it is showing up in this process? What is the Process Consultant's role here to facilitate learning?
4. If growth in programs, staffing, and mergers is off the table, what kind of strategy is this organization looking for? In what way do the Process Consultant and planning team need to learn together? Who facilitates that learning? Who seems responsible to put any learning to use?
5. What potential landmines do you sense in this strategic planning process? How might any of these steps derail? How might the attempt at transparency with staff backfire?
6. After so much growth in programs and success in fund raising, how might the board be dissatisfied with an approach that the organization needs a "time out" to digest all this growth?

2. Foundational effectiveness?

Background. A foundation dedicated to regional impact in educational attainment awarded grant funding to six universities to create and deploy a student scholarship and support program. The goals of the program were to expedite degree completion among traditionally under-represented students and to help students avoid student loan debt.

While meeting basic guidelines, each university was allowed to customize the programming to meet the needs of their students, combining scholarship dollars with interventions such as mentoring, group meetings, financial literacy, career workshops, and individual advising for the scholarship recipients. This combination of financial support, professional advising, and peer-based activities was a hallmark of the program.

The foundation also invested in a long-term evaluation of the program that included significant collection of qualitative and quantitative data through a quasi-experimental design, all to be analyzed and reported on an annual basis. The evaluation team took a Process Consulting approach and was able to adapt with the Client through staff turnover, unforeseen challenges in data collection, and the disruption of education due to the pandemic of 2020-2021.

The findings of the evaluation were statistically significant in many areas such as grade point average, matriculation, and degree completion. However, the foundation did not have a plan to disseminate the findings beyond close stakeholders such as board members, grantees, and influential partners. The positive findings could help influence decision-makers in school districts across the state, in university administration, other educational grant makers, and state legislators who were changing the landscape of high school design with little data about effectiveness.

In addition, it was discovered that university administrators who were responsible for managing the programs had informally been reaching out to each other to "compare notes" and exchange their experiences about student outcomes, program implementation challenges, and opportunities to use program lessons to benefit the larger population of similar students on their campuses. In response, the foundation created an annual study meeting for foundation staff, grantees, and the evaluation team to share lessons learned.

The evaluation team and foundation staff agreed that as the program continued to grow, they needed a plan for how to share complex information across multiple constituencies who may or may not have knowledge about the program and its effectiveness. The foundation also saw an opportunity to transform beyond the role of strategic philanthropists into thought leaders in the sector. The foundation and evaluation team decided to work on a dissemination plan together.

PROCESS DESIGN

Why **are we doing this?** The scholarship program was highly successful and there was an opportunity to help others who support vulnerable students by sharing lessons learned from the evaluation. The foundation was committed to continuous learning but was humble in its approach to sharing success.

Who **plays what role as we address this?**
- The foundation and the evaluation consultants formed a task force among their team members to focus specifically on the development of a dissemination plan that honored the foundation's desire to put the focus on grantees as the "heroes" of the narrative, with the foundation being a supporter.
- The evaluation consultants served as advisors based on previous experience and created a rubric to document progress toward a final plan.
- The foundation's marketing and communication consultants reviewed the plan and offered insight based on the foundation's larger communication efforts.
- Grantees were included as potential speakers, presenters, and convenors in their region.
- The task force agreed that any presentations or written articles should include at least one grantee to represent the actual implementation experience.
- Where the audience might be researchers, the task force agreed that at least one member of the evaluation team should be present.

What **criteria will help us measure success?**
- Completion of the dissemination plan that clearly identifies core messages, target audience, attention-worthy topics, and a schedule of potential events, conferences, and publications to which to submit presentations, findings, or papers.
- Commitment from foundation staff members, evaluation team members, and selected grantees, including budget for time and travel.
- Documentation of accomplishments toward goals.
- Long-term, inquiries to the foundation, grantees, or evaluators from interested parties wanting to learn more about the program.

When **do we wish this work to be completed?**
- The task force agreed to complete a draft of the dissemination plan within a 4-month period and scheduled meetings specifically on this topic, outside of other evaluation meetings.
- The plan was then circulated to grantees and the communications firm for their input with revisions made over a 2-month period.
- The final plan was ready to implement 6 months from the start.
- The pandemic hit just as the plan was completed and the task force was able to provide only one virtual conference presentation in the original timeline. The team adapted and decided to focus on written materials such as topical briefs and articles.

Where **will this work take place?** There was one one-person meeting held at the annual study meeting where the learning community could discuss and respond to the plan. The remainder of work occurred remotely via phone, email, and videoconferencing.

How **will we complete this work?**
- The group gathered existing evaluation findings and identified opportunities for dissemination and gaps in research that may be of interest to external audiences.

- The group gathered lessons learned from grantees beyond other evaluation deliverables, to capture what was top-of-mind for them and what they thought other higher education officials or scholarship providers may want to learn about.
- Collectively, the group created detailed personas of the type of influencers they were hoping to reach and crafted talking points and core messages; some were practical in nature for school district leaders or college admissions and retention staff, and some were technical for the research or policy community.
- The task force worked in a draft and response mode whereby the evaluation team offered first drafts of documents, the foundation responded with suggested edits, and the evaluation team finalized the dissemination plan.
- The plan was summarized in a spreadsheet to easily manage the process and progress toward goals.

—Kim Stezala

FOR PROCESS CONSULTANT DISCUSSION

1. This case study reflects a completed process. Where do you think this process held great alignment among stakeholders and where do you think things did or could go wrong?
2. Drawing on Kohlberg's six stages of development considered in this chapter, at what level are the Process Consultant and Client organization functioning? What might a higher level of functioning look like?
3. What parts of the case study exemplify learning in partnership towards transformation and adaptation?
4. While this is a simplified composite of several evaluations, many Clients overlook the power of dissemination to spark discussion and learning, or to transform organizations or systems. What examples do you have where Clients are reluctant to embrace a more public voice, or conversely, ready to transform and share their story?

The Tenth Core Competency

LEARNING TOWARD WISDOM

Learning in Partnership concluded with the foundational idea of ongoing upward and outward personal and organizational development. A learning partnership needs this common direction for both the Process Consultant and the Client.

The Process Consultant is pursuing their own ongoing personal transformation, and from this vantage point partners with the Client as they both awaken to what next makes for ongoing organizational and personal transformation. This builds the possibility for the Client's remaining "on mission," the Client's sustainability for the long-term, and the possibility of the Client becoming or remaining a learning organization.

In more recent works by Clare Graves,[43] the Danish scholar Lene Rachel Andersen, and others, there has been a significant attempt to organize how the many fields of development (e.g., personal, organizational) come together and toward what end. One outgrowth of this work is the Bildung Rose,[44] which we recommend to any Process Consultant seeking a robust and integrative development model.

Out of these many models one element needs to be made more explicit.

THE TENTH CORE COMPETENCY

The Process Consultant and Client need to keep transforming toward wisdom. For this we draw on Lene Rachel Andersen and Tomas Bjørkman's book *The Nordic Secret: a European story of beauty and freedom* [45] rather than the more dated Kohlberg model shown in the previous chapter.

A best practices Process Consultant capable of exercising the Core Competencies of Process Consulting would reasonably be expected to be a self-governing person (layer three as seen in Figure 18 below). Their personal and vocational experiences can lead them to a layer four choice of professional freedom over professional security and to establish a consultative practice. As they grow their self-authoring choice (layer four), they have opportunity to move more deeply into a self-transforming layer (layer five) as the aspirational mission, strategy, and goals of their Clients become the center of the Process Consultant-Client trust relationship, especially where Client objectives touch the creative, sustaining, and resilient needs of a flourishing world.

A Process Consultant who moves into the self-transforming layer must understand that they will encounter persons who operate in or move back and forth between all five of these layers. They will work with organizations that function lower than the fifth layer. The Listening competencies of the Process Consultant must take this into account so that Helping and ultimately Learning can be mutually constructed and engaged, becoming sticky and impactful, not just for the Client, but for the larger world.

This is where triple loop learning[46] comes in.

Figure 18 The Layer	The Process Consultant	The Client Person	The Client Organization
Layer One Self-Discovering	Legally Compliant	Recognizes rules and avoids penalties. Unaware of future implications of past or present actions	Incorporated. Functioning ethically and legally
Layer Two Self-Consolidating	Vocationally Experienced	Aware of self-interest and discovers how to contribute. Individually distinct and aware of relationships	Intentionally organized and market-facing with a specific product/service mix
Layer Three Self-Governing	Lifelong Learner. Masters their area(s) of expertise. Prefers vocational freedom over security	Seeking inter-personal and sustained relationships. Desires to be trusted and valuable. Meaningful rather than transactional relationships	Governed by mission, vision, and values Operating Systems in place
Layer Four Self-Authoring	Curates learning as new knowledge and contributes to their Clients and colleagues	Chooses their role and how they will contribute. Seeks to contribute distinctively and bring an individual and leadership voice for the benefit of others. Self-determining	Organizational culture and leadership development. Strategic and scenario planning. Operational excellence pursued
Layer Five Self-Transforming	Moves knowledge toward wisdom and contributes to the flourishing of the world beyond their lifetime	Identifies systems and sub-systems that are dependent on wise action. Gives self to a purpose beyond one's own lifetime	Multi-scenario planning, long-term and future value building, legacy, and succession planning with the flourishing of others in mind

Figure 18

Whereas organizational learning can take place in any loop as diagrammed below (Figure 19), a learning organization consistently engages in triple loop learning. Accordingly, a competent Process Consultant should be able to construct and layer single, double, or triple loop process with a receptive Client, as needed, while remaining clear on the differences between them.

THE TENTH CORE COMPETENCY

Please note that the right to left looping movement of **Mission<—Policies** in the diagram loosely corresponds to the five development layers in the above section. Notice, too, that it is difficult to engage triple loop learning without being in touch with the uniqueness of a context.

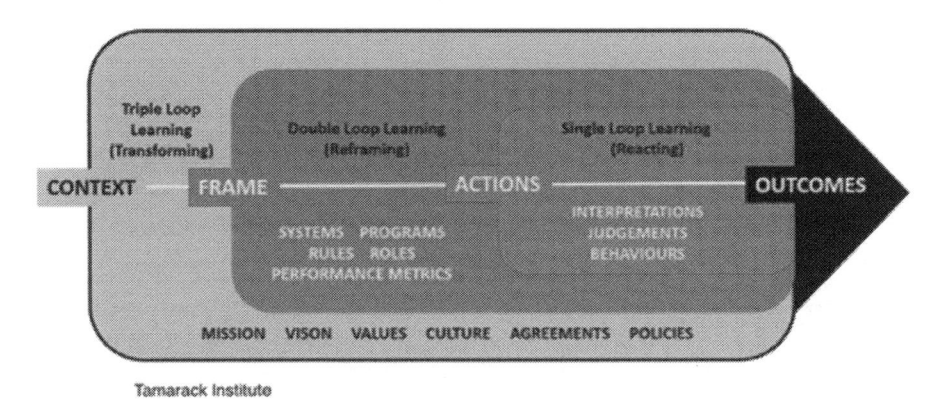

Figure 19

RESULTS—Presenting Issue, Pragmatic Need
LOOP ONE—Behavior Change, Action, Doing
LOOP TWO—Underlying Issue, Framing, Reframing, Thinking
LOOP THREE—Perceiving, Discovering, *"What do we have here?"* Systems Effects, Adapting, Transforming

---

Client organizations that engage in triple loop learning do not ignore the need for the actions and results of Loop One or the benefits of describing and framing in Loop Two. Rather, triple loop learning helps the organization move forward in a virtuous and momentum-building cycle, revisiting and re-articulating their mission, vision, and values yet again.

Let's look at this from the other side also. Triple loop learning processes shorten the path of resistance to change. Triple loop learning puts change management at the front end of the process where Client ownership and alignment can be developed, rather than at the end when change management all too easily becomes Client personnel forcing and selling each other internally.

Triple loop learning makes it more possible that adaptive moves will last and be built upon.

Process Consultants will seek to grow their competence in designing, following, discovering, implementing, documenting, and celebrating the needed triple loop process in partnership with their Client.

WISDOM GROWS OUT OF TRIPLE LOOP LEARNING

Client wisdom, more often called organizational wisdom, grows out of intentional triple loop learning. Organizational wisdom has been defined as *the collection, transference, and integration of individuals' wisdom and the use of institutional and social processes (e.g., structure, culture, leadership) for strategic action.*[47]

The Turkish scholars Ali Ekber Akgun and Sümeyye Yücebilgilli Kirçovali wrote a paper in 2015 titled *Organizational Wisdom and Its Impact on Firm Innovation and Performance.*[48] They suggest that organizational wisdom can be modeled as the *virtuous and prudent practices* of the organization (that which is within the organization's control to do) in order *to innovate* in environmental uncertainty (adaptive moves). which has some *bearing on the organization's financial performance* (financial performance does not rest entirely upon organizational behavior or control but it matters).

The assumption here is that virtue and prudence should be built up and transferred into a repository of people in addition to organizational policies and systems. But how is wisdom built up, recorded, and then transferred? We are brought back to the first two ideas of this chapter:

1. The *intention to be self-transforming* for the benefit of the world after one's own lifetime. Stated more simply for vocational and organizational life: to do transformative work that benefits the world after one has fulfilled their role.

THE TENTH CORE COMPETENCY

2. The *use of triple loop learning* so that perceptions can be adjusted, adaptive moves attempted, discoveries made, and the world advanced in sustainable ways—doing so that future generations have this same opportunity.

Building and retaining organizational wisdom is often hard-won, especially when working with a Client marked by lower layer behaviors (layers one, two and three). The Process Consultant's familiarity with change management models such as ADKAR[49] are needed to be able to help a Client move toward lasting, triple loop learning.

> A — Awareness of the need for change
> D — Desire to support the change
> K — Knowledge of how to change
> A — Ability to demonstrate new and skills and behaviors
> R — Reinforcement to make the change stick

Please notice how each letter in ADKAR roughly corresponds to one of the five levels described by Andersen and Bjørkman, above. Please note, also, that it is difficult to reinforce a change if key players remain unaware that change is needed, or that they are aware but do not have desire to change or knowledge of how to do so. When knowledge is lacking it cannot become wisdom that can be reinforced. When a Client is ready for knowledge acquisition adaptive moves become possible— something well beyond a technical fix.

The Process Consultant can engage in self-reflection here. How easily do they themselves move from awareness of need for change and then to reinforcing the changes they discover would add to their own transformation? How might they wisely use their self-reflection insights to foster empathy for the Client who is on this this same journey toward wisdom?

LANDING ON THIS CORE COMPETENCY

Accumulated wisdom can be passed along if those receiving it are also open to reflection and ongoing transformation. Wisdom is something people and organizations grow toward, should they choose to do so. They cannot do this if they are not opened to reflect, to learn, and then to transform as they adapt to what is discovered. This level of learning marks the service of the Process Consultant.

Learning toward Wisdom
CASE STUDIES

1. Acquiring Co. seeks an acquisition

Background. Acquiring Co. is a lower-middle market machine tools manufacturing company without previous experience in business acquisitions. Acquiring Co.'s principal owners, the President and Chief Financial Officer, recognize that Acquiring Co. is not meeting consistent sales growth targets in current markets or with current customers, despite quality products, proactive sales and marketing efforts, and strong customer relationships. Rather than retrenching or waiting for the situation to improve, Acquiring Co.'s executives choose to consider possibilities for sustaining and growing their businesses through mergers or acquisitions.

Acquiring Co.'s executives contacted their trusted attorneys, accountants, and banker, asking how they could best prepare, learn about, and gain expertise in acquisitions. These advisors explained the significant complexities of acquisitions and the dozens of skills needed, including valuation, accounting, tax, legal, government regulation, negotiations, due diligence, equity and debt structuring, integration, and all their subsets. Acquiring Co.'s executives appreciated that their existing team of skilled advisors and a respected investment banking firm (M&A Advisor) will work together to support and handle details of the acquisition process and help Acquiring Co. concentrate on its core activities while acquiring a new business.

PROCESS DESIGN

Why **are we doing this?** The M&A Advisor asked the owners what they were looking for. At this point, Acquiring Co's primary acquisition criteria was "to grow 15% annually through acquisitions." They asked M&A Advisor to show them whatever opportunities M&A Advisor came across. When M&A Advisor asked if they would know a good match when they saw it, they admitted they might not. M&A Advisor explained, "To be successful, we need to know what you are looking for and how you expect that to improve your business. If you can honestly describe and share who you are as a company and your vision of who you want to be coming out of this acquisition, we can help develop good search criteria for what acquisitions will most profitably enhance your business. This foundational description of your company and strategy will both help you find and match good acquisition candidates, and help candidates understand why Acquiring Co. might be a good fit for them too. Do you have this description or someone who can help you with this?" They did not have an internal M&A team or a consultant to help them discover and clarify their strategic objectives, and M&A Advisor recommended a qualified Process Consultant.

Who **plays what role as we address this?**
- Consultant will help Acquiring Co. follow and complete a discovery process to identify, develop, and describe both who Acquiring Co. essentially is (mission, values, and culture) and the company's vision, growth objectives, and strategies for the future.

- M&A Advisor will use Acquiring Co's acquisition criteria and strategic objectives from the discovery process to research, surface, and pursue dozens of good strategic acquisition targets and ask their owners to consider a new opportunity for positive reasons beyond price. Then M&A advisor will assist Acquiring Co.'s team with introductions, confidentiality agreements, meetings, sharing information, negotiations, financial analysis and other diligence, valuations, deal and financing structures, compliance issues, and so on.

- Acquiring Co.'s executives will be integrally involved in critical decision-making, defining vision and acquisition criteria, learning about potential products and businesses, evaluating fit with acquisition targets, financial analysis, planning offer terms, due diligence, and integration.
- Acquiring Co's law firm, accounting firm, and bank will work expeditiously with M&A Advisor on legal, tax, financing and financial diligence matters, and structuring, negotiating, and documenting the transaction.

***What* criteria do we look at to know that we succeeded?**

- The discovery process with the Process Consultant will accelerate a learning process about activities that are keys to future success of Acquiring Co., particularly helping to develop specific focus areas, priorities, goals, and strategies for the next three years for both organic growth and growth through acquisitions. Acquiring Co's leaders will be aware of their assets and strengths and where they need more knowledge and will assign teams to work on these areas. A smaller leadership team will work with consultant and M&A Advisor to essentially describe the company, overall growth plans, and acquisition criteria. Acquiring Co's leaders and teams will broadly reinforce and share modifications to its mission, values, vision, and objectives for organic growth and implement them.
- To expand learning and help strengthen Acquiring Co's culture, the discovery process will generate involvement, enthusiasm, and energy among participants. The objective is to involve as many

contributors as possible in discovering, describing, celebrating, and sharing Acquiring Co's mission, vision, values, culture, hopes, dreams, and objectives with a view to improving and strengthening the future of the company. Acquiring Co's leaders and the Process Consultant will determine who needs to be invited to be part of the process. The process will include reporting back to participants and getting additional feedback.

- The discovery process will help Acquiring Co's leaders and teams working on negotiations, diligence, or integration matters identify key practical, strategic, and cultural attributes to evaluate in their interactions with acquisition candidates.

When do we wish this work to be completed?
- The description of the company, growth plans, and acquisition criteria will be in usable form for M&A Advisor within 90 days so M&A Advisor may begin identifying qualified potential acquisition candidates to contact with AC's approval.

- Implementation of organic growth goals will begin within 120 days and follow timelines specified in the goals. Additional goals may follow as teams complete more work or identify additional priorities.

- The goal is to complete an acquisition within six months after surfacing interested acquisition candidates.

Where will this work take place? Initial planning with the leadership team will take place in the consultant's conference room. Planning and training with the larger leadership team and department heads for the discovery process will take place on a full day scheduled for two weeks from now. Small group and team meetings will take place in the small conference room at AC's facilities or by Zoom. A meeting with the larger leadership team and department heads to review and analyze the results of the small group meetings will take place one week following.

How **will we complete this work?**

- The Process Consultant will introduce the process and hold Appreciative Inquiry approach conversations with small groups of executives and department heads, take notes from these sessions and, at the same time, train participants to schedule and lead these conversations with other small groups of employees throughout the company and to take notes in these sessions.

- The sessions will be completed and all notes will be collated within 30 days.

- The larger leadership team will meet with the consultant to identify and discuss common observations, experiences, themes, values, opportunities, and objectives, as well as potential focus areas, priorities, and goals for the next three years (in comparison with goals AC already has for the business).

- Participants will discuss where the company has assets and strengths and where they need more information, research, or development (especially in products, marketing, sales, manufacturing, and human resources) and what teams to assign to follow up on these questions. They will discuss how particular participants could help on some teams as well as what to report back to all participants and get feedback on.

- A smaller leadership team will work with consultant and M&A Advisor to essentially describe the company, overall growth plans, and acquisition criteria. Leaders and team liaisons will meet with consultant to share information and revise and continue their work. Parts of this process may be somewhat constrained by a perceived need not to broadly announce acquisition plans.

—Jim Gettel

THE TENTH CORE COMPETENCY

FOR PROCESS CONSULTANT DISCUSSION

In what ways is the Process Consultant helping AC to gain wisdom to use in completing a successful acquisition and grow its businesses?

1. In reading this case study, where do you experience optimism that this could have a good outcome, and where are you concerned?
2. What questions might you ask to further flesh out the context, develop an architecture for a healthy process, and uncover potential landmines?
3. How would the end of this process be described by those involved: Strengthening the company through a discovery process involving many people? Preparing for a successful acquisition by creating a good match through discovery, diligence, and integration? Beginning an ongoing relationship and organizational development process?

2. Double whammy

Background. _____ is a non-profit US organization with a head office in western Europe. It is an established organization that partners with close affiliation to an international subsidiary. The partnership represents four decades of continuous collaboration in mission and vision. The complexity of globalization and long-term efficacy for both entities are substantial as is true for many non-profit organizations world-wide.

The present and existing challenge is the succession of senior leadership transitioning into retirement within the next 2-5 years, presenting significant organizational and personnel changes. Loss in historical knowledge, expertise and leadership capacities are apparent concerns. A quadrennial assessment and review reveal that the current organizational structure needs refinement and refocus of shared values to secure long-term sustainability.

The partner organizations retained a Process Consultant to design a viable structural plan for leadership succession and facilitate necessary discussion on re-identifying shared core values.

PROCESS DESIGN

Why **are we doing this?** Each Council Board faces the challenge of efficacy in accomplishing its mission. It functions well in the short-term, but with the apparent changes in leadership and personnel, the loss of vision is at risk. There is no long-term sustainability.

Considering the partnership and close affiliation between the two organizations facing a similar challenge, a collaborative opportunity is presented. Each Council Board would like to have a process in place for leadership succession suitable for their unique context.

The intention to develop and equip emerging leaders is a constant desire. The wisdom, experience and expertise of the current leadership is an asset to the future of the organization. The transference of wisdom and historical knowledge to the next governing council would be an invaluable process

Continuing to operate with a less effective strategic plan yields low performance long term. An innovative learning partnership dialogue would be apropos in this time of transition.

Who **plays what role in the process?**
- The Council Boards and Advisors of both non-profit organizations are the decision-making bodies. The two Council Boards combined seat 13 members and 5 advisors who govern and lead the organizations.

- The Process Consultant will facilitate the needed discussions among the Council Board and Advisor members focusing on re-identifying shared core values and awaken needed change. It will be a parallel learning process.

- The Process Consultant, in collaboration with each Council Board and its Advisors, will construct a relevant and viable structural plan for leadership succession. The partnership between these two Boards provides opportunity for a sharing of resources and expertise; therefore, this will be considered.

- The work will be supervised by the Council Board Chairman of each organization. Each Chairman will communicate any major changes directly their boards.
- The assistance of an International Attorney may be needed for international legal issues.

What are the criteria for success?

- Increase capacity of members to reflect and understand present issues that impacts the viability of the organizations.
- An openness to consider a learning partnership with the purpose of personal and organizational transformation.
- Ongoing education and development of members present and future.
- Maintenance of strong communication and transparency in the structural design process.
- Openness to consider the collaboration of resources between the two Council Boards.
- An outlined process of leadership succession including next steps by end of next quarter.
- Continued and increase clarity of:
    –Long-term mission and vision of organization.
    –Shared values between partnering organizations.

When is the desired work to be completed?

- An outlined process of the structural plan for leadership succession (including next steps) will be determined by the end of next quarter.

- Proposal for necessary funding be processed and approved by April 30th for fiscal year beginning July 1.
- The intended date for completion of the work is before the next quadrennial which begins two years from now.

Where **is the work being conducted?** The initial dialogue will take place during the annual leadership meeting in the month of September at a designated location. The Process Consultant will have quarterly virtual meetings with the Council Boards and Advisors.

How **is the work proceeding?**
- The Council Boards will retain a Process Consultant for the design process.
- The Process Consultant will work with the Council Boards to grow in understanding of the current structure and document discussion topics to consider in the design process.
- The Process Consultant will facilitate the annual leadership meeting in September to re-identify shared core values and develop a collaborative roadmap.
- The roadmap will outline specific and sequenced steps to pursue in the next quarter and identify key participants.
- The Process Consultant will collaborate with each Council Board to design a leadership succession structural plan suitable for their organization by facilitating engagement from current leadership. Quarterly and/or biannual meetings will be scheduled as needed to evaluate plans.

—Celine Bower

FOR PROCESS CONSULTANT DISCUSSION

1. In the structure of this Process Design, where do you identify organizational learning taking place? Where might wisdom come into play beyond mere institutional knowledge?
2. What levels of personal and/or organizational development would be unprepared to address the complexity offered in this case study? Why?
3. What would be the definition of collaboration between these two organizations? Is it already a shared definition? How do you know?
4. How would you measure long-term organizational sustainability? Do you think the Client in this case study shares that measure with you? How would you gain assurance that you share the same meaning?
5. What might be the desirable outcome for these two non-profit organizations? How would you remain facilitative as you worked with this Client rather than telling them what they need to do?

The Eleventh Core Competency

LEARNING TO EXCHANGE

This Core Competency, as established by the Society for Process Consulting's Standards and Ethics Committee, defines *exchange* as *Expectation to share (leak) knowledge and insight so others can flourish*. The definition continues by pointing out that learning and then exchanging fosters even more co-learning that will also be exchanged. At its base is an expectation that learning and exchange will be abundant and collaborative.

An exchange intention is an abundance intention. Learning to exchange is a "give first" orientation. An exchange intention holds the belief others will contribute in return, thus making it possible for us all to make even better use of what will be learned in the future. An exchange intention knows that others may choose not to participate, may fail to learn, or may discard what was offered, with knowledge becoming lost. It perseveres in giving away, picking up something new to make something of it, and then giving that away, and so on. It holds a conviction that the net effect of more being learned and retained than learning that is lost brings the possibility of hope for others who come after us.

Learning to exchange is also transformational. The adaptive process that is the trade of the Process Consultant, when generously and mutually distributed, invites the Process Consultant and the Client to keep growing and giving.

By contrast, *a proprietary intention is a scarcity intention.* A proprietary intention holds learning back and tries to secure it out of (reasonable) fear that what is already known will be lost or stolen. A proprietary intention protects knowledge from pirates, disaster, or decay.

A proprietary approach produces or replicates knowledge and then limits access, protecting and encasing it into something that can be sold or licensed. The proprietary intention is transactional. Rather than using the adaptive process as their trade, a Subject Matter Expert makes a technical product out of their knowledge: accumulating knowledge, securing it, offering exclusive use of it for a price.

A practical comparison between an abundance and a proprietary intention is the difference between open-sourced and closed-source software. Another example is the difference between a community with thoroughfares and common areas such as parks versus a gated community that keeps all passersby outside the fence. We might also consider the difference between a World Bank that publishes a knowledge repository intended to leak globally and a manufacturing corporation that spends thousands on security software so that their engineers' drawings cannot be stolen by industrial pirates.

An abundant, "give first" exchange of learning happens on the following levels:

- *Inward exchange,* with self.
- *Outward exchange*, among colleagues and the Client.
- *Forward exchange*, for past and future Clients.
- *Onward exchange,* to the flourishing of the world.

The progression of these four exchanges is ever outward, from self at the center to the world's flourishing as the outer concentric ring.

INWARD EXCHANGE WITH SELF

How should we understand an inward exchange with self? It is as simple as understanding that you cannot give something away if you don't acknowledge that you have it or if you refuse to put it to work. Acknowledgement and appropriation at a personal level is necessary if knowledge is to be shared outwardly with others.

Here is a for instance. If a Process Consultant refuses to embrace knowledge of learning styles when they develop a training presentation, and if they insist that Client participants must adapt to the Process Consultant's preferred form of transmitting information, that Process Consultant will not be able to demonstrate (exchange) information with all the Client participants. They also will not be able to learn from their Clients, some of whom could be even more advanced in their ability to train according to learning styles. A Process Consultant not engaged in lifelong learning stops learning, so no exchange with self takes place, and neither does an exchange with others.

OUTWARD EXCHANGE WITH COLLEAGUES AND CLIENTS

When a Process Consultant is open to learning and has an open and generous-hearted listening posture and helping partnership, they can then have a learning service through the outward exchange with Colleagues and Clients. The:

- processes they design,
- data they gather,
- frameworks they create,
- insights they gain,
- reports they prepare
- knowledge they curate, and
- the wisdom they uncover adds to the well[50] of what can be drawn upon repeatedly as new work and new adaptive moves happen.

Again, we are brought back to acknowledgement of what is learned and used. The power of asking *What do we have here?* helps this exchange take place naturally. The Process Consultant (with their colleagues) and the Client remain shoulder to shoulder just as they were when developing a Process Design, and just as they will be when an adaptive move is implemented.

FORWARD EXCHANGE FOR PAST AND FUTURE CLIENTS

A forward exchange with past and future Clients comes when the Process Consultant or the Client uses their acquired knowledge elsewhere.

Previous experiences can be part of framing new and future processes. They can inform:

- questions with subsequent Clients that help to frame the issue for the new Client.
- steps a Client declares they intend to take, and some of the possible directions they might pursue.

Further, this type of exchange puts the Process Consultant in an excellent position to connect future with past and current Clients. This is a value-add for the Client engagement as the Client has occasion to engage with peers and to consider possibilities they might not otherwise easily come across. These conversations are extremely generative: beneficial for the current Client, the past/present/future Client, as well as for the Process Consultant. Let's not forget that satisfied Clients cannot help but tell others, not just about who helped them, but what the help was, thus potentially shortening the transformation cycle for potential Clients.

ONWARD EXCHANGE TO THE FLOURISHING OF THE WORLD

An extra-Client exchange sets the stage for further, onward exchanges that help the world to flourish.

The Process Consultant learns and is learning and thereby can exchange what they've learned.

- as a part of their business development activity,
- in their co-learning alongside their Clients,
- in the curation of what is learned among colleagues and new Clients,
- on and on in a virtuous cycle.

Colleagues and Clients benefit from this learning because of the eco-system that a Community of Practice provides. A carefully curated platform makes it possible for knowledge to be exchanged with others when the originator of that knowledge is not even present. Examples include inbound marketing, distribution of white papers, listening to a podcast, or even one Client sharing what they've learned in a subsequent presentation some years distant. No one Process Consultant can talk to thousands of people in ways that are meaningful and remained rooted in Client-defined and Client-owned solutions. Letting knowledge leak, permitting it to be exchanged, does make it possible.

Clients who tell potential Clients what they learned, combined with a curated repository of information, make for exponential exchanges of knowledge that can be built upon further.

BILDUNG AGAIN

Let's close by returning to Bildung as a source for this exchange perspective. Bildung holds the idea that we give ourselves to continue growing while making it possible for others to grow. By contrast, if you search the internet for the phrases "knowledge leak" or "knowledge exchange" almost everything you find will be about keeping knowledge secure and protecting it from prying eyes. The overwhelming fruit of such a search is about others not benefitting unless they pay. Knowledge gets monetized by selling, licensing, or servicing intellectual property. This vast effort keeps knowledge from the Commons.

While the Commons are assets that we share such as roads, parks, and libraries, the Commons are also knowledge that is widely disseminated. In the Bildung approach to the Commons, we grow what is available in the Commons and the wider spreading of our contribution for everyone's well-being.

An example of this difference can be seen in the COVID era. Proprietary approaches to facemasks can be found in those that are sold because they are fashionable, practical, or hygienic. For example, balaclavas are seeing a resurgence in sales because of their practicality as facemasks. The Commons approach are the now ubiquitous no-touch hand sanitizers and paper masks available as you enter restaurants, stores, and congregations.

This perspective helps the Process Consultant enter a Client relationship as a transformed and as an ongoing self-transforming person, more able to spot where transformation might happen with the Client, and with grace and patience to help others discover and step into their transformation. It is a Commons approach because the Process Consultant is offering this exchange in the first and in all subsequent conversations. Those who do this work professionally repeatedly make available their artful, efficient, wise, and practiced approach to Process Design and facilitation, regardless of any advanced technical knowledge they might possess. And they do so prepared to help others, especially within a Client engagement so the Client can begin to develop its Process Consulting skills. The Process Consultant does not lose as they do this because they keep moving further up and in with their practice. What they know is not threatened by others learning to do the same because the competition is not other successful and skilled Process Consultants. The competition is chaos, ignorance, malaise, and fear—that which would destroy the enduring organizations we seek to serve, and the flourishing lives we want to enable.

CONCLUDING THOUGHT

An exchange of knowledge should not be seen as a return to "telling" and being a Subject Matter Expert. What is advocated with this competency is a wise use of what is known and what is in front of us to discover. The Process

Consultant does not withhold knowledge as that would prevent discovery. Neither do they impose knowledge as that circumvents the Client's learning process and threatens the Client's own exchange with self.

The Process Consultant uses their knowledge to help frame the Client's approach to an adaptive challenge and provides safety and certainty so that everyone involved has opportunity to co-learn even more than they know already. "Telling" assumes a complete knowledge and short-circuits the triple-loop learning described in the previous chapter.

Learning to Exchange
CASE STUDIES

1. What business are we in now?

Background. Food & Finery is a regional, boutique kitchenware and cooking store that's facing another strategic juncture. Founder Myrland Meyer established the business as a small town, single location mercantile store in the 1940s, and under the long-term leadership of his daughter Marcia, the business grew in both product focus and geographical breadth to what has been for several decades now a high-end kitchen goods store with a strong regional footprint throughout the Northeast U.S.

Marcia's children Jillian and Alec have been leading the company as CEO and COO, respectively, for roughly 20 years. They've focused on augmenting in-store products and purchasing with an online sales and wedding registry program, and more recently expanded to include on-site cooking studios and classes. The business experienced exponential growth across all

3 segments—in store, online, and now cooking school—to coincide with dramatic market growth in cooking and kitchen-centered homes.

But now, Food & Finery is seeing significant declines in both its onsite and online businesses, due to dramatic increases in online purchasing at the expense of in-store, and a David-versus-Goliath market dynamic online that finds them competing against high-profile national competitors with expansive inventory and strategic wedding registry partnerships. Only their cooking studio has remained strong, and even that is slowly regaining steam again after months-long pandemic shut-down.

Jillian and Alec are wondering if it's time to sell or transition the business in some way. They've enlisted the help of a Process Consultant to help them assess this honestly and objectively. And if there is merit in continuing the business in some form, they find themselves wondering, *What business are we in now?*

PROCESS DESIGN

***Why* are we doing this?** Jillian and Alec are concerned about continuing erosion of the business. Their family has had an enduring commitment to the communities they serve: being a go-to, accessible resource for goods and services; serving as a trusted partner for generations of local families for wedding gifts and family holiday and gatherings; investing profits back into the community through education and nonprofit giving and sponsorships; and more recently, offering studio cooking events that allow families to gather together, videotape a matriarch or patriarch as they make family-favorite recipes, and preserve these experiences for future generations and posterity. They've focused on growing the business with a strong stakeholder, rising tide lifts all boats mindset; and have enjoyed mutual, win-win partnerships with their vendor partners.

They've experienced two years of declining revenue, and as they kick off what looks to be a third —as trends point to continued erosion—their goal is to use these next 6 months to honestly assess the current and future state of the business; identify any trends where they have business equity and could potentially focus, reinvent, and capitalize; or whether it's time to sunset or sell the business in some way. They would then use the next 6 months to create and operationalize an action plan.

Who **plays what role as we address this?**
- Jillian and Alec are ultimate decision-makers but realize that family legacy has implications for how/when to involve extended family in the decision process.
- Marcia, their mother—now in her early 80s—has not been actively involved in the business for years but has a strong vested interest and influence in whether the family business legacy continues and in what form.
- Jillian and Alec both have kids in their teens who are too young to commit to future interest in the business, but they wonder whether/how to involve them in this process given the strong family legacy.
- The Process Consultant will facilitate the process, helping Jillian and Alec develop a road map that includes business evaluation, market trends, stakeholder insights and input, and strategic decision-making, and considers how/when to involve the broader family in the process.
- The Process Consultant may enlist strategic expertise in key areas of research and analysis if capacity issues and time constraints arise.

What **criteria do we look to know that we succeeded?**
- A preliminary, go-forward business decision at the end of 6 months and resulting operational plan developed and ready 6 months thereafter.
- A process roadmap that incorporates:
    - Sources and analytics needed to inform decision-making.

– Identification of key stakeholders--for both input and insights-gathering, and for proactive communication at key decision junctures.

– Appropriate communications touchpoints and strategies for key stakeholders.

- Ultimately, a go-forward decision and plan that honors the business realities/potential and considers Food & Finery's strong stakeholder relationships and active participation in its communities.

When do we wish this work to be completed?
- Jillian and Alec would like to share their recommendation to key stakeholders 6 months from today.
- The research and analysis roadmap will detail steps toward learning and insights over these next 5 months.
- The Process Consultant will schedule strategic updates throughout that five-month process and will facilitate a strategy and decision-making retreat for Jillian and Alec between the fifth and sixth month, to begin processing in earnest all they've learned and translating it into a recommendation.

Where will this work take place? The work will be based at Food & Finery's corporate office, with research and analysis conducted both in-office and in-market. Final analysis will be reviewed, and a strategic recommendation developed at an offsite 2-day retreat at a location to be determined.

How will we complete this work?
- The Process Consultant will work with Jillian and Alex to develop a roadmap that honors and reflects their company's longstanding commitment to learning from and alongside key stakeholders to best serve their current and emerging needs.
- The Process Consultant will lead and facilitate the steps identified

in the roadmap, as well as reporting in on findings at key junctures to ensure that Jillian and Alec are learning and considering insights/options throughout the process.

- The Process Consultant will schedule and facilitate the offsite retreat, where Jillian and Alec will process the findings in earnest and develop their go-forward recommendation.

—Kristin Evenson

FOR PROCESS CONSULTANT DISCUSSION

1. Many scenarios like these contain elements of "set down" as well as "carry forward." What do you see Jillian and Alex setting down and what do you see them carrying forward? Do they seem to be missing anything? What discovery questions might the Process Consultant ask of them?
2. What exchanges of knowledge and wisdom do you find in this case study? What might enhance or hinder this exchange?
3. Does this Process Design get at the underlying issue or issues? What would you add or adjust to this Process Design?
4. What can Alex and Jillian control here? Where do they merely have influence and what is beyond their ability to control? Are they functioning at a high enough level that they are thinking beyond themselves to the benefit of others? What more might they do and how might facilitated conversation help them discover it?

2. Competing for space

Background. In Milwaukee, oftentimes, all the local homeless shelters are at capacity for the winter months. Even more concerning, the need to shelter women and children keeps growing without any winter shelter space available. As a temporary solution, homeless individuals are sheltered in warming rooms within churches and community centers, though it's clear these solutions are not sustainable. In response, MilCats, a local foundation, invited five community-based organizations (CBOs) focused on homelessness to come together to tackle the need for additional winter shelter in the city. Tired of throwing together temporary fixes, stakeholders committed to working together to find a lasting solution.

To create a stronger collaboration, MilCats is providing each of the five nonprofit partners with $10,000 for the staff time to participate in a series of meetings. However, when the diverse group of stakeholders, comprised of executive directors, front-line staff, and individuals with lived experience come into the same room, it isn't long before each of them is jockeying for the floor, hopeful that their idea will win out over the others. There are whispers amongst the nonprofit leaders present that the foundation will give significant seed money to the solution, but nothing has been confirmed. With this underlying assumption, the nonprofit representatives are more focused on how their organization can get more "face time," and there is little effort made to collaborate.

After being together for only one hour, there is a feeling in the room that everyone wants to rush the decision. Some ideas have been offered, but those with lived experience of homelessness bring up the lack of innovation. The ideas presented offer minimal support required, not going far enough.

Tensions rise as people begin talking past each other, more concerned with being heard than with listening. People begin to feel defensive. This dynamic becomes more apparent when programs from the past are questioned, even attacked. People begin to feel hesitant to share because others may steal their ideas. There is a fear that if they are genuinely collaborative, another nonprofit may reap the benefit of additional foundation funding from MilCats and possibly other funders. They even begin to ask themselves, *Could my current funding be in jeopardy?*

Ever present in the room, MilCats quickly noticed the worsening dynamics and sensed that if they didn't make a change, distrust would only continue to mount over the coming months. They needed support in facilitating the process. After a pause to regroup, MilCats retained a Process Consultant to facilitate the rest of the process. Together they would design a strategy to open more winter shelter by November 1st, six months into the future.

PROCESS DESIGN

***Why* are we going this?** MilCats Foundation has observed a trend year after year: nonprofit partners come to them for *last-minute* grants to provide *temporary* winter shelter options to the unhoused. From their perspective, they do not think that any of the current solutions are viable long-term. MilCats is willing to convene nonprofit leaders and those with lived experience to formulate a long-term solution. In six months, they will take the project from strategy to implementation.

***Who* plays what role as we address this?**
MilCats Foundation convenes a group of stakeholders to participate in the process. Utilizing an equity lens to drive the process, the foundation intentionally assembles individuals of diverse backgrounds and perspectives to be at the table. It's deemed necessary to have individuals with lived experience of homelessness present and for their time and unique knowledge to be compensated equitably. In total, a group of 18-21 stakeholders are identified:

- As the lead conveners, MilCats Foundation has two program staff who will participate in the process. Their voice is to be included in the discussions. Whatever solution may arise, they will have the option to present a funding request to their foundation, but there is no guarantee. Final approval would need to be received from their board of directors, but the two staff wield significant influence on the process.
- Three other local foundations have been invited to participate in

the process. Each is asked to have one or two designated representatives join the conversations. There is an understanding that there will need to be additional funding sources for long-term solutions to be sustainable. Unlike MilCats Foundation, there is little guarantee that these additional foundations will provide funding.

- Two representatives from five different nonprofits have been invited to be a part of the conversation. Each individual should hold a leadership role within their organization and should have the authority to present ideas from this team directly to senior leadership and/or the board of directors. Nonprofits will receive $10,000 each to participate.

- Three individuals with lived experience of homelessness have been asked to join this strategy team. Their experience is valuable to developing a strategy and plans for implementation. Each individual will be offered $500 each month to participate ($3,000 each total for six months or up to $9,000 if each individual participates the entire time).

- In addition to the stakeholders listed above, the Process Consultants will facilitate the conversations and will map out the solutions presented. Two consultants will be involved.

    –One Process Consultant will focus on facilitating the meeting between the various parties.

    –One Process Consultant will focus on strategy and, while present during all the meetings, will be focused on being a part of the implementation team.

What criteria do we look for to know that we succeeded?
- A winter emergency shelter to be open by the first of November.
- A strategy will include input from all participants.

- As trust is built in the process, there will be a consensus within the group as to the next steps.
- Funding has been secured.

When do we wish this work to be completed?
- By July 1st a consensus has been made to the strategy to move forward.
- By August 1st MilCats board of directors will approve a set amount of money to be used as seed money based on the consensus arrived at by July 1st.
- By September 1st approval has been made by any nonprofit partner involved in implementing the plan.
- By November 1st the winter shelter will be open.
- Re-evaluation for next winter will begin in February. While the first meeting will include all current team members, the team may include other individuals who have become involved in the process over the last year.

Where will this work take place? The MilCats Foundation offered their meeting rooms at 123 Meax Place for the first three months of meetings. After the first three months, the meetings may be transitioned to the location of the winter shelter if room is available. If not, MilCats Foundation will continue to make space available. Sub-committees may choose to meet virtually or at a mutually agreed upon location.

How will we complete this work?
- The Process Consultants will work with the team to guide the process over the next six months. While some of the meetings will stay consistent, there will be smaller groups meeting as needed throughout the process.
- The Process Consultants will focus on developing more trust/

better collaboration that will hopefully continue after this process in less formal ways.

- During the first meeting, MilCats will bring to the group the possible parameters of funding moving forward.
- The team will meet two times per month for the first three months. Each meeting will be 2 hours in length.
- Each month the Process Consultants will work to make sure all voices are heard, including ensuring that individuals with lived experience are able to participate fully in the work.
- As the strategy is being developed, small groups of members may meet to fill out details between meetings.
- In the month of July and August, the process will move from theoretical strategy to planning execution. The strategy will create a structure, define goals, and assign tasks for moving into implementation.
- Once approved by both MilCats board of directors and any nonprofit partners utilized in execution, meetings will begin focusing on implementing the strategy.
- Facilitated meetings will take place twice a month through November and then monthly through February.
- The February meeting will focus on debriefing the implementation of the winter shelter and reviewing the process taken.

—Catherine (Draeger) Pederson

FOR PROCESS CONSULTANT DISCUSSION

1. What issues may arise when bringing together a diverse team to solve the problem of the need for winter shelter? Where might they agree,

and where might they differ? How might they move more toward exchange and co-opetition and away from acting as competitors? How might exchange arise among them?
2. Why do you think it becomes difficult for this group of individuals to be opened to sharing their resources and expertise? How open-minded do you think members of this team will need to become to risk sharing information which may benefit a related nonprofit in the future, specifically when it comes to future fundraising efforts?
3. Is it the Process Consultants' responsibility to stay neutral or removed from the process? What if the discussion moves to the point of feeling transactional and not transformational? Is it the Process Consultants' role to guide discussions of values and guide discussions of strategy and implementation? What if the discussion touches on subjects in which the consultant has previous experience?
4. Check in with yourself as you consider this case study and its Process Design. What is happening in your body, your thoughts and in your emotional center? Why do you think this is? How might what you notice influence your approach to this case were you the Process Consultant working with MilCats?

The Twelfth Core Competency

LEARNING FOR POSTERITY

Consider this: fewer than 20% of companies have succession plans.[51] Even fewer have a plan for developing, stewarding, and passing along organizational knowledge. Failure to plan for succession and continuity almost assures that the current value of an organization is all that it has, and that even that will not be fully passed along. It almost ensures a diminishing value with each passing period of measure.

Consider also that 60% of the USA population does not have a will.[52] Even fewer people have estate plans, a designated power of attorney, or trusts. This almost assures that these estates, even if just a few items and a small bank account, will disappear through final medical expenses, court probate fees, and, if there is any money available, through the spending of heirs.

Legacy, in its simplest form, is to make a gift of what one has. Posterity goes further, thinking to the furthest generation. The intentional posterity we might want to have is first and foremost harmed by our failure to plan. Posterity is secondarily harmed by individuals who receive a legacy but are not yet prepared to receive it. These individuals are also not thinking about a contribution of their own legacy that in turn will be made accessible for others, and so on toward posterity.

This short-term, me-centered, give me *my* shot approach consumes wealth rather than creates it for others' benefit. Process Consultants and Clients come together to work out organizational and leadership problems, often growing from this limited and erroneous perspective. They will not be able to work their way out of the problem by putting short-term thinking on problems that grew out of short-term thinking. This limited framework blocks creativity to build and maintain current value, let alone pass value along as a foundation for the future.

Legacy and posterity happen. Either we are intentional with our gifts, or we are not. Either we decide to whom these are given and when and how, or someone else decides for us. Related to this, our control of who receives it, when they get it and how they use it, is minimal. The more control we try to exert, the more disappointed we will be. And the more control we try to exert, the more control we remove from others to add to that legacy.

The Self-Transforming Layer (Layer Five) as iterated by Andersen and Bjørkman (Figure 18 in the Core Competency of Learning Toward Wisdom) is where posterity is considered and valued. Posterity is not just an adult consideration of the long-term effects of one's actions. It is the transformed consideration of the long-term effects of everyone's actions on everyone in all time frames, and not just on people but the systems and sub-systems in which they live.

Quoting Lene Rachel Andersen in her 2020 book *Bildung: Keep Growing:*

"If we do not grasp what is going on in all the <u>domains</u>, we are not empowered. If we cannot contribute to the production and provide for ourselves; if we cannot use the latest technology appropriately; if we cannot make decisions based on the latest science; if we cannot develop ethics that allow us to make appropriate choices in unfamiliar situations; if we cannot pass on our cultural heritage; if we cannot appreciate the arts and aesthetics that expand the collective symbolic world— then we cannot remain in power over our own life." (p.123)

Figure 20	The Process Consultant	The Client Person	The Client Organization
Layer Five Self-Transforming	Moves knowledge toward wisdom and contributes to the flourishing of the world beyond their lifetime	Identifies systems and sub-systems that are dependent on wise action. Gives self to a purpose beyond one's own lifetime	Multi-scenario planning, long-term and future value building, legacy and succession planning with the flourishing of others in mind

Figure 20

We can add that if we are not in power over our own life, then we are not able to offer posterity a legacy that others can pick up, understand, use, and build upon. Even more, when we fail to engage and apply lifelong learning with freedom *and* responsibility, then we remove power over the lives of future generations. We diminish legacy and harm posterity. We become Bildung robbers rather than its contributing creators.

The previous section identifies the decisions we make toward posterity: deciding upon *who*, *when*, and *how*.

For the Process Consultant:

Who:

- Clients past, present, and future, helping them also transform toward posterity awareness and action
- Colleagues past, present, and future, transforming with them toward posterity
- The world and its flourishing

Thomas Paine is widely quoted as saying that when we plan for posterity, we are wise to keep in mind that virtue is not hereditary. His sentiment is even more reason to understand that careful succession, when planned and enacted, contributes to legacy and posterity.

Succession is *who*. Who is coming along behind the Process Consultant to pick up on ongoing Client relationships and to build upon what has been

THE TWELFTH CORE COMPETENCY

learned? Have we been witness to the development and employment of virtue among those coming after us? Or do we just hope that whoever picks up what we set down will know what they have and use it virtuously?

Succession, legacy, and posterity are part of a Process Consultant's practice from the beginning. This is not something one "gets around to" but is constantly on the alert for. The timing of succession will be when the *who* can be identified far more than *when* the Process Consultant decides they are personally ready to step away.

When:
- In real time (Now)
- Continuous
- Whenever successors (Who) can be identified
- Lifelong and longer

How
- Intentional residual and/or equity relationships[53]
- Online knowledge repositories — curated and searchable
- Group e-mail/messaging
- Peer-based review
- Collegial gatherings with informal and formal opportunities to share knowledge, especially via case studies
- Society for Process Consulting credentialed training[54]
- Onboarding activities specific to a Community of Practice

A more specific and final *who*, *when* and *how* comes at the end of one's career, or perhaps earlier at a key gateway when the Process Consultant is narrowing, expanding, or transitioning their practice. Succession, Legacy, and Posterity become far more concrete in such a moment. How well that concrete sets depends on how the Process Consultant deliberately worked to build, curate, and exchange knowledge all along.

Examples of acting toward posterity and doing it well is scant. The few examples of doing it well are built on at least two best practices. First, planning for posterity from the beginning and keeping any succession plan up to date. This applies both to the Process Consultant for their individual practice as well as any formal platform from which they conduct their practice. Secondly, rigor and clarity about one's own roles and domain, especially when transition is underway and the Process Consultant has not completely stepped away from their practice. We are Process Consultants after all. Our ability to manage our own succession and continuity testifies to the depth of our skill. Even more, our doing it well grants us increased capacity to Listen, Help, and Learn alongside Clients who want to build something that endures.

Learning for Posterity
CASE STUDIES

1. Jonesy's succession

Background: Jonesy's, a midwestern US farm implement and supply yard owned by the Smith Brothers (their mother was a Jones before she married), represents four generations of continuous family ownership. They are working on a succession plan for the fifth generation of this business, recently valued at $45 million US.

Each brother has one son. These first cousins who have a twenty-year age gap between them will each receive half of the business. Henry, the older cousin, has worked at Jonesy's all his life and runs the supply yard. Jim, the other cousin, was raised by his mother in a different state. Jim is fresh from his MBA at an Ivy League school and will move to the area during the holiday season.

Henry and Jim are polite, tense, and uncertain of each other. The Smith brothers remain confident that the cousins will overcome their awkwardness and that any misunderstanding will work out as it always did between them. The brothers are eager to wrap up succession planning and move into retirement, already visibly disconnecting from day-to-day operations as they feel their time coming to an end. They retained a Process Consultant to develop and then facilitate the steps to move succession successfully forward.

PROCESS DESIGN

Why **are we doing this?** The Smith Brothers wish to retire at the end of the current fiscal year for estate tax and health reasons, passing ownership and all operations to their sons. Estate plans, legal documents, and a financial structure are prepared to maintain a 50-50 ownership between the cousins. *Continuing to operate the business under the cousins' leadership has not yet been developed and needs to be.* Titles, job descriptions, incentives, and compensation structure, conflict management procedures, further expected development in executive leadership, the appointment of any advisory or corporate board, any ongoing role of the brothers, and the actual handing over of the keys is not yet determined. Three months remain before year-end and the intended date of ownership transfer.

Who **plays what role as we address this?**
- The Smith brothers are final decision-makers but realize most everything that now needs addressing must have contribution and ownership from their sons who will succeed them.
- The Process Consultant will facilitate the needed discussion among the brothers and cousins, helping them design a road map

and sequence of steps to continue operating the business while developing Henry and Jim's executive leadership capacity and confidence.

- Any ongoing professional assistance, including the possibility of retaining a strategic interim general manager for an as of yet unidentified period to help manage the transition, will be specifically identified in the road map.

- Henry and Jim's spouses are on record with the Smith brothers that they want this well-planned so that their home life need not be stressed by business matters or any future relationship conflict between the cousins. All four men agreed in advance that the Process Consultant should have some backchannel conversation with the daughters-in-law before meeting with the brothers and cousins so that their perspectives can be honored.

- The corporate attorney is on call to quickly draw up any needed documents that detail job descriptions and any bylaws that might reflect an advisory or governing board, should that be one of the determinations.

- All estate, investment, and banking matters are designed and ready to be signed but await the landing of some of the specific transition and operational plans.

What criteria do we look to know that we succeeded?

- Wrapping up the transfer of ownership by 30 December of the current year.

- A road map agreed to by all parties that they can imagine and are eager to live into, can be expressed as a working covenant, develops the executive leadership capacity of new ownership, and remains flexible to adjust and keep updated as insight is gained and any amended actions emerge.

- The four men end the next fiscal year as fathers and sons, confident that they made a good decision and acted honorably for all concerned, especially employees, customers, and their respective families.

When **do we wish this work to be completed?**
- The intended date of ownership transfer and submission of all related documents is midnight, 30 December, so it is reflected in the current fiscal year.
- This gives ninety days to develop the road map the Process Consultant will help fathers and sons put in place.
- The road map will identify steps to take through the first three quarters of the next fiscal year. One essential step already identified is a monthly meeting between the cousins working on their relationship and communication strength, using an outside facilitator.
- The road map needs to include an evaluation meeting with the Process Consultant in August of the following year, specific date TBD, to inform the next round of annual planning.

Where **will this work take place?** There is one enterprise facility located at 2468 Jonesy Place and is the business for which ownership will be transferred. The road map will largely be completed during an October weekend at a rented lodge.

How **will we complete this work?**
- The Process Consultant will work with the structure in place thus far and the guiding principles of this Process Design to develop an initial draft of a road map the brothers and cousins will work from in developing the road map.
- The Process Consultant will facilitate the October weekend with the fathers and sons to develop the roadmap and draft a working covenant.

- The roadmap will develop specific and sequenced steps to follow in November and December as the final steps toward ownership transfer occur.

- The roadmap will outline a sequence of specific steps followed after the transfer of ownership and toward what the fathers and sons define as a successful first year.

- Facilitated monthly meetings after the transfer of ownership will focus on the working relationship and communication between the cousins.

- A meeting by the end of August in the next year will evaluate the first year and lay the groundwork for plans in the next fiscal year.

—Mark L. Vincent

FOR PROCESS CONSULTANT DISCUSSION

1. What seems to be the definition of posterity among the brothers and cousins in this case study? Where are they in agreement, and where might they differ? How open do you sense they are to continue learning and for whose benefit?
2. In reading this case study, where do you experience optimism that this could have a good outcome, and where are you concerned? What questions might you ask to further flesh out the context, develop an architecture for a healthy process, and uncover potential landmines?
3. How would the end of this process be described by those involved: A hand-off from the current generation? A successful first year for the next generation of ownership? Preparation for a sixth generation to come? Something else? How would the end they are expressly pursuing influence the steps they will take and how they will take them?

THE TWELFTH CORE COMPETENCY

2. A giant tree is falling

George Brent Tomàs opened his computer to write an email to a Process Consultant who had served him and his company well a little over ten years previously:

Dear Henrietta,

It's been a while hasn't it! Your work with us all those years ago bore a lot of fruit for what was then our little forestry operation. Your help in making mission, vision, and values meaningful and at the center of all our decisions has helped us build an operational maturity as well as develop some future executive leaders.

I thought we would call on you for some additional projects since then, but at each turn what you taught was so effective that we found ourselves developing a strong bench of in-house people with ready-to-use Process Consulting skill. This really showed up these past couple of years with all the wildfires here in the northwest. We began working with large-scale, state-level service contracts that brought about 300% growth in the last five years. We worked together to develop a brand that combines fire prevention with cleanup and reseeding. We even moved into a partnership with one state university to strengthen their forestry program that now includes graduates serving in the Amazon, Sumatra, and Central Europe.

You had considerable and lasting influence on us then, and I'm hoping to call on you now if you are available. All those years ago you taught us to make consistent use of Process Design using why, who, what, when, where and how questions. I'll use those questions below, to help you understand what needs to be done now.

Why am I writing to you? *I have a lung condition that gives me at best a three-year prognosis for living. Even if I live a little longer than that, I will deteriorate considerably along the way, probably needing to be on oxygen all the time a year or so from now.*

LEARNING FOR POSTERITY

My estate planning and powers of attorney are all updated and in place, but I remain the sole owner of the company. We need to get a successor in place soon, or at least a qualified interim CEO until a successor can be found. This will also likely mean we need to finally put in place a board of outside directors. I'll be glad to give you additional background if you agree to take this on, but an ESOP or a sale would not be preferred courses of action at this time. My current goal would be to turn the business over to a trust that would be governed by a Board of Directors according to a charter I've begun to draft. In fact, it was drafting the charter that brought you to mind.

Who would do what? *I would like to work with the two of us to start, drafting the set of steps we would follow across the next six months to get most of this done. We can draw in my attorney, the estate planner who has been so helpful to me, and others as needed. I realize this is an accelerated timeline, but even still it is of such necessity I am prepared to pay what it costs to do this well and thoroughly.*

What success criteria do I want to achieve?

- *All of this in place and begun in the next six to nine months so that I am alive to see it! What we cannot accomplish needs to have a well-laid out set of next steps that I feel are moving us along.*
- *That we have done all we could within our power for ensure an enduring enterprise.*
- *A successor (or interim) in place, guided by a strong and experienced Board of Directors who represent the Trust according to its charter.*
- *An ability to step away completely within a year so I can spend my last months surrounded with family and friends.*

When *will we do this work?* *I should have focused on this long ago but did not. So, "yesterday" is the best answer. If you are not available for what I believe would be a fairly intensive push across the next six months, I'd welcome you tapping your network for someone whose skills match yours.*

Where *will this work take place?* *I am still able to travel so I'll come to you if necessary. However, I'd like to give you an updated tour of our operational center and equipment yard at our main site, at least. I think we would meet in person for a couple of days to get a robust plan in place, and perhaps to complete the draft of a charter for the Trust. I'm open to your suggestions, of course.*

How *would we proceed?* *Once I have a yes from you, we would set a date to meet ASAP. The sequence of steps from there would be something for us to develop together.*

Henrietta, if you are not available for this I will certainly understand. Hopefully I've conveyed a calm urgency here.

I eagerly await your reply. Offered with my thanks,

George Brent Tomàs

—Mark L. Vincent

FOR PROCESS CONSULTANT CONVERSATION

1. Thinking about the Learning competencies, where can you identify Partnership, Wisdom, Exchange and Posterity within this case study?
2. The next steps in Process Design would likely flesh out a scope and sequence of a successor search and recruitment of a Board once a Charter is in place. How would you begin laying this out? How much of it this work would require professional assistance from others and

how would you go about retaining them? What if Henrietta was not available? How do you think she would go about making a qualified referral? If you were Henrietta and were not available, would you be able to make a qualified referral? How could your current network come into play with this story?
3. Given your experiences with scenarios like these, where have you seen success and where have you witnessed failure? What do you think would have turned those failures toward success?
4. If you found yourself in a similar situation as George Brent Tomàs when it comes to your Process Consulting Practice what would your letter to a trusted advisor say?

A FINAL WORD

And now we are full circle. We return to *why, who, what, when, where,* and *how*.

Once we listen and help alongside a Client, the most effective way to make the results of learning visible and available . . .

- In Partnership
- Toward Wisdom
- To Exchange
- Toward Posterity

. . . is to keep growing in clarity and artistry as we form Client Agreements and facilitate Process Design.

Looking back and searching for curated examples, case studies, and moves that adapt and innovate, a future Process Consultant or a future Client can easily uncover why something mattered so much, who played what role in figuring it out, what was the criteria of success, and then when, where, and how it was handled. Research for future innovative and adaptive moves can be simplified, and future process is made more efficient and effective. Future frameworks for expeditious facilitation with a Client; deeper expertise in one's field; wider expansion of networks; greater impact on systems and sub-systems; and ongoing organizational and personal wisdom enriches the Commons[55] within the field of Process Consulting and to the world beyond.

The idea of posterity is ancient. It reaches back to the beginning of time and then forward to generations we will never see. The ancient Hebrews said it this way in one of their hymns written in the middle of excruciating suffering, a reason one faces to the future even when all seems a reason to despair:

Posterity will serve him; future generations will be told about the Lord (Psalm 22:30).

The Buddha, writing at about the same time, is reported to have had a vision that the wisdom he was conveying would last five hundred years.

We are told that the philosopher Plato's chief reason for writing down the teachings of Socrates was for the purpose of posterity—for the use of future generations beyond his lifetime.

From these longstanding examples we are reminded that the Core Competencies of the Process Consultant are for the flourishing of the world long after we are gone, and this something far greater than the current or next Client Agreement.

ENDNOTES

1. Design Group International. *About us,* https://www.designgroupinternational.com/about-us, 2020. Accessed 8 October 2021.
2. wwww.societyforprocessconsulting.com
3. *Wheel Forward or Spiral Downward*, Design Group International, https://www.linkedin.com/pulse/wheel-forward-spiral-downward-making-choice-strategic-mark-l-/, accessed 16 October 2021.
4. Hartmann, Jack. *Be a whole-body listener,* https://www.youtube.com/watch?v=pQ77Nr6TgZo, 2018. Accessed 8 October 2021.
5. The Empowerment Dynamic. *WAIT: Why Am I Talking?* https://powerofted.com/w-a-i-t-why-am-i-talking-2/, 2015. Accessed 23 October 2021.
6. Joseph Shaffner. *Why am I still talking? WAIST—the lost art of listening,* http://www.northrockleadership.com/w.a.i.s.t.html, 2020. Accessed 22 October 2021.
7. If the Client already fully comprehends their problem (or believes they do) and approaches the Process Consultant to bring expertise to the Client's already defined solution, they are approaching the Process Consultant as a project manager, a contractor, or a vendor, which is different than a Process Consultant.
8. When asked *Is there anything else?* Clients often respond with *No,* but then proceed to provide more information or additional stories. It is often not until asking *Is there anything else?* several times that the Client says, *We can't think of anything more.*
9. Jason Sample, Echo Listening Profile: *Effective Communication for Healthy Organizations,* https://productionkeywords.s3-us-west-2.amazonaws.com/uploads/uteodi4sr/sample_echo_profile_9_22_18.pdf, 2018. Accessed 15 August 2020.
10. It is advisable to review the Client Agreement with the Client at each Client interaction.

11. Ovidijus Jurevicius, *SWOT Analysis: How to do it Properly*, https://strategicmanagementinsight.com/tools/swot-analysis-how-to-do-it/, 2021. Accessed 31 October 2021.
12. Dr. Fong Chun Cheong, *Environmental Scanning and SWOT analysis*, http://www.hkiaat.org/e-newsletter/Mar-18/technical_article/PBEII.pdf, School of Business, Macao Polytechnic Institute. Accessed 31 October 2021.
13. Dr. Thomas Vande Zande, *A Three Step Guide to Immersing Yourself in the Future*, https://www.flagshipfutures.com/blog/a-three-step-gide-on-immersing-yourself-in-the-future, Flagship Futures, 2019. Accessed 31 October 2021.
14. Mark L. Vincent, *Multi-scenario planning: Not Just in Emergencies*, https://www.designgroupinternational.com/mark-l-vincent-blog/multi-scenario-planning-not-just-in-emergencies, 2020. Accessed 25 May 2021.
15. Arnaud Chevalier, *Triangulate on answers*, https://powerful-problem-solving.com/triangulate-on-answers/, 2011. Accessed 10 October 2020.
16. In my experience as a Process Consultant, I've found triangulation among the most powerful of tools in the toolbox. One quick illustration to show its usefulness: I've worked with several boards of Client organizations struggling to set a salary for a chief executive. These boards wanted to do a salary comparison in order to gain guidance for determining what compensation level to offer. That was the presenting issue. The underlying issue for these boards is that did not have active personnel or executive committees who conducted reviews and set salaries on an annual basis. They had no point of reference and opinions about what a salary should be were uninformed, subjective, and varied. Board relationships with these executives were becoming strained. Triangulating information helped reset a baseline for compensation and set the stage for the even more needed conversation about strengthening their governance. We triangulated by:

- Going back to the compensation package offered when hiring the current executive, then working forward via an inflationary adjustment.
- Gathering data from similar-sized organizations in the same region, finding the median of the compensation ranges.
- Gathering data from similar organization that serve the same industry, finding the median of those compensation ranges.

ENDNOTES

The resulting information shows the range of difference (if any) between the compensation of the chief executive (had it kept pace with inflation) and that of the triangulated, far more objective data. The boards then made informed and wide-awake decisions about compensating and retaining the executive they have, as well as being more prepared for recruiting when needed in the future.

17. Chip Wilson, *Trusting your Gut is the Best Business Tool You've Got if You Can Listen,* https://www.forbes.com/sites/chipwilson/2018/06/14/trusting-your-gut-is-the-best-business-tool-youve-got-if-you-can-listen/?sh=219f069a4b16, 2018. Accessed 12 October 2020.
18. Maya Angelou, *We Hear You,* https://www.youtube.com/watch?v=CND2M-lCRJ0, 2014. Accessed 1 November 2021.
19. Emotional Regional Learning Consortium, *What is a Community of Practice?* https://www.communityofpractice.ca/background/what-is-a-community-of-practice/, 2016. Accessed 1 November 2021.
20. By definition Process Consultants cannot be directive. They do not have role authority and they are not necessarily in the facilitative role because they are the most expert person on the Client's "it." Instead, the currency of the Process Consultant is trust:

    - that they have worked hard to understand the Client and the Client's context.
    - that they have each person's dignity at heart.
    - that they want to see the Client organization fulfill its mission according to its guiding values.
    - that they are patient, reliable, steady, and a co-learner beside the Client.

21. Philip C. Bergey and Mark L. Vincent, *Organizational Development Consulting: We Might Turn You Down, https://www.designgroupinternational.com/mark-l-vincent-blog/theorganizationaldevelopmentmuse/bid/104457/organizational-development-consulting-we-might-turn-you-down,* 2011. Accessed 7 November 2021.
22. https://www.linkedin.com/in/barryovereem/, accessed 20 August 2020.
23. Kim Stezala, Mark L. Vincent, *Wheel Forward or Spiral Downward: Making a Choice for Strategic Design,* https://f.hubspotusercontent40.net/hub/113048/file-16554083.pdf, accessed 28 November 2021.

24. The Nobel Prize winner, Daniel Kahneman calls this "competitive spite" in his book *Thinking Fast and Slow.* Farrar, Straus and Garoux, 2011, p. 210.
25. Shahab Shahib, *Corpus Collosum,* https://www.kenhub.com/en/library/anatomy/corpus-callosum, accessed 27 August 2020.
26. The Process Consultant does not necessarily know what the Client is coming to know. Even if they do know the best answer already, it is not critical that the Process Consultant shares Client knowledge. They are not primarily a subject matter expert, a vendor, or a contractor. It is the ability to guide a co-learning process that is the trade of the Process Consultant because they are experienced in journeying through to learning. The Process Consultant, therefore, does not lead with knowledge and answers, but with wisdom and questions that fosters a Client's insight beyond what either of them know at the start.
27. If a Client is not listening to themself or their context, they are not centered. A Client-centered Process Consultant cannot help if the Client is not focused or willing to become so.
28. Human Resource Development Press, 1993.
29. See Etienne Wengerd's discussion on Alignment in ch.8 of his book *Communities of Practice: Learning, Meaning and Identity,* Cambridge University Press, 1999.
30. This diagram is part of the larger Maestro-level leaders initiative of Design Group International (www.maestrolevelleaders.com). The diagram is often used to identify where organizational or executive leadership capacity needs further development.
31. PROSCI, *Organizational Change Requires Individual Change,* https://www.prosci.com/methodology/adkar, accessed 7 December 2021.
32. Tom Frick, *Our Problem Framing Template,* Mightybytes, https://www.mightybytes.com/blog/problem-framing-workshop-template/, accessed 23 December 2021.
33. Kay Edwards, *Market research might not be the luxury you think it is,* Convene Corp.,https://www.convenenow.com/blog/market-research-might-not-be-the-luxury-you-think-it-is. Accessed 20 October 2020.
34. Arnaud Chevalier, *Triangulate on Answers,* Powerful Problem Solving, https://powerful-problem-solving.com/triangulate-on-answers/, Accessed 24 December 2021.
35. Pavel Kukhnavets, *The Meaning and Power of Weighted Decision Making in Business,* Hygger, https://hygger.io/blog/weighted-decision-matrix-in-business/, Accessed 24 December 2021.

ENDNOTES

36. Liz Finney and Carol Jenkins, *Best practice in OD evaluation: understanding the impact of organisational development,* roffeypark, https://informalcoalitions.typepad.com/odin/Roffey_Park_OD_Evaluation_Report_Exec_Summary.pdf, Accessed 1 October 2020.
37. Forbes Coaches Council, *11 assessments every executive should take,* Forbes, https://www.forbes.com/sites/forbescoachescouncil/2018/05/01/11-assessments-every-executive-should-take/?sh=2b08ca167a51, Accessed 3 March 2021.
38. *Customer experience (CX): the guide to customer success,* https://www.i-scoop.eu/customer-experience/, Accessed 12 December 2021.
39. Cynthia Vinney, *Kohlberg's stages of moral development,* Thought Company, https://www.thoughtco.com/kohlbergs-stages-of-moral-development-4689125, accessed 26 December 2021.
40. Steve Thomasen, *Robert Kegan: the five orders of consciousness,* Prezi, https://prezi.com/yave1wdy4p_l/the-five-orders-of-consciousness-according-to-robert-kegan/, accessed 18 September 2020.
41. Sven Erik Nordenbo, *Bildung and the thinking of Bildung,* Journal of Philosophy of Education, vol. 36, no.3, 2002, http://armytage.net/pdsdata/Bildung%20and%20the%20thinking%20of%20bildung.pdf, accessed 26 December 2021.
42. Mark L. Vincent, *The three turns of executive leadership*, Maestro-level Leaders, https://www.linkedin.com/pulse/three-turns-executive-leader-mark-l-vincent-phd-epc/, accessed 4 September 2020.
43. Psyche Games, *Spiral Dynamics,* https://www.fruitsinfo.com/psychegames.com/spiral-dynamics.htm, accessed 27 December 2021.
44. Lene Rachel Andersen, *The Bildung Rose,* http://bildungrose.com/, Nordic Bildung, Accessed 15 January 2021.
45. Lene Rachel Andersen and Tomas Bjørkman, *The Nordic Secret: A European story of beauty and freedom,* Fri tanke, 2017.
46. Tamarack Institute, *Single, Double, and Triple-loop learning, https://www.tamarackcommunity.ca/hubfs/Events/Multi-Day%20Events/Community%20Change%20Institute%20-%20CCI/2017%20CCI%20Vancouver/Resources/Tool%20-%20Single%20Double%20Triple%20Loop%20Learning.pdf,* accessed 14 August 2021.
47. Bierl, Kessler and Christensen, 2000, Organizational learning, knowledge and wisdom. Journal of Organizational Change Management, p.601.
48. https://9lib.net/document/

myjed1kq-organizational-wisdom-impact-firm-innovation-performance.html, Doğuş Üniversitesi Dergisi, 16 (2) 2015, 193-202, accessed 27 December 2021.
49. Prosci, The Prosci Adkar Model, https://www.prosci.com/methodology/adkar, accessed 7 July 2021.
50. "Well" is a fun word that essentially means platform. The platform of a best practices Process Consulting Community of Practice should keep a confidential, secure, backed up, curated, searchable repository of learning. At a minimum, it can include Client Agreements, Client Reports, Client Findings, related case studies, content generated as blogs, podcasts, videos, white papers, and more. It should NOT include private or proprietary Client data unless storing that Client data is explicitly part of the Client Agreement.

    Talking about a repository of learning as secure is somewhat ironic since Process Consulting Core Competencies expect knowledge leaks and exchange. Still, what belongs to the Client is the Client's. What belongs to the individual Process Consultant by way of intellectual property is the Process Consultant's. And what belongs to a Community of Practice is that Community's. The Core Competency being described here is about giving away what one learns, not taking learning away from others, while making it less possible for the learning of others to be stolen.
51. Peter Greer, *About Succession*, https://www.peterkgreer.com/succession/, accessed 14 September 2021.
52. Barbranda Lumpkins Walls, *Haven't done a will yet?* https://www.aarp.org/money/investing/info-2017/half-of-adults-do-not-have-wills.html, accessed 13 September 2021.
53. By tying succession to a financial model, Process Consultants are financially incentivized to care about legacy and posterity—whether they are departing or entering the profession.
54. www.societyforprocessconsulting.com
55. http://www.onthecommons.org/about-commons, accessed 4 January 2021.

CONTRIBUTORS

PHILIP C. BERGEY, PhD, PCC, EPC, is an executive coach, Process Consultant and educator. Through Design Group International, he helps leaders transform themselves and their systems. Building on more than 30 years in board and executive leadership in business and non-profit leadership settings, he attends to results and relationships with humor, flexibility, and depth.

CELINE BOWER worked with non-profit organizations in Europe and Middle East for the last 17 years. She maintains a posture of learning in the areas of leadership development, cultural intelligence, and culinary arts.

VICKI BURKHART is founder and CEO of the More Than Giving Company, which helps volunteer-driven nonprofits succeed through strategic and capacity planning, board/leadership development, and innovative staffing solutions. She has 30+ years of experience in the nonprofit arena as an Executive Director, nonprofit executive, and consultant.

GRETCHEN COLÓN, MBA, CFRE, lends hands, heart, and wisdom to purpose-driven organizations. She recently partnered with long-time collaborator, Alex Stelzer, on a startup focused on literacy through the use of process consulting. Gretchen helps develop communities through branding, marketing, communications, generosity, board development, team building and coaching.

KAY EDWARDS has spent her career helping values-driven leaders find clarity in complex times by helping them listen to their customers and understand what they are really saying. She founded Outsight Network with the vision to help clients and consultants do more of what the world most needs them to do.

JOHN ERICKSON has a background in engineering, the US Foreign Service, higher education, and leadership development. **Dennis Humphrey** spent the last 30 years as a mental health professional helping people understand themselves, get unstuck, and make better decisions in their lives and relationships. Together, they own Eden Consulting, working with business leaders and their organizations.

KRISTIN EVENSON spent 20 years with Fallon Worldwide, leading brand and communications strategy for clients such as Nordstrom, Holiday Inn Express, and Children's Defense Fund, winning multiple national effectiveness awards. Now working with CEOs, teams, and boards, she helps them navigate strategic junctures by leveraging their unique brand of significance.

JAMES C. GALVIN, Ed.D., is an organizational consultant focusing on strategy, governance, and leadership development. As an author, Jim has been published by Zondervan, Tyndale House, Thomas Nelson, Baker, NavPress, Moody Press, and InterVarsity Press. He is also the co-creator and senior editor of the best-selling Life Application Study Bible.

JIM GETTEL, coach and consultant, helps church and nonprofit leaders discover effective ways to lead loving, fruitful communities that make a difference in the world. Jim successfully served clients and built organizations as a lawyer, corporate and nonprofit executive, investment banker, congregational development officer for two Episcopal dioceses, and consultant.

JENNIFER MILLER is a Fractional Chief Marketing Officer and Owner of Strategically Connected. An experienced marketing leader and Process Consultant, she managed and built sales and marketing teams from the ground up. Her passion to support and build scalable processes led to receiving the honor of the #1 Fastest-Growing Technology company in Austin and #86 on the 2019 Inc 5000 list.

CATHERINE (DRAEGER) PEDERSON, Ph.D., is the CEO of Loving Venti Consulting Practice. Recipient of a Ten Outstanding Young America's (TOYA) award from the United States Junior Chamber (Jaycees), and the Philanthropic 5 award from United Way of Greater Milwaukee and Waukesha County, she earned her Ph.D. in Leadership, Learning, and Service from Cardinal Stritch.

DEANNA ROLFFS, EPC, is a Process Consultant, strategist, facilitator, coach, and systems thinker, working with executives and teams. Her Process Consulting approach focuses on organizational transformation via thriving teams, brave leadership, equitable systems, and inclusive communities. Deanna writes about her messy journey in her blog: *Leadership and Learning Letters*.

CARLOS ROMERO serves as Administrator and Vice-President of Operations at Hamilton Grove, a Greencroft Community, a 260+ acres Continuing Care Retirement Community in New Carlisle, Indiana. He previously served 17 years as the Executive Director of the Mennonite Education Agency.

ELEANOR SCARLETT, CPC, is ordained in the United Church of Canada and a designated Intentional Interim Minister passionate about transitional work. She is a member of the Credentialing Committee and the Social and Ecological Justice Commission of the UCC. A Process Consultant, and a Conflict Resolution Officer, she serves on the Board of the Interim Ministry Network.

KIM STEZALA M.S., EPC, is CEO for the Society for Process Consulting. She has devoted more than 25 years to nonprofit, education, and business sectors in management, volunteer, and founder roles. She is dedicated to educational access, specifically the pipeline to and through college. Kim is known nationally as The Scholarship Lady®.

LON SWARTZENTRUBER, M.A., MBA, ACC, EPC, is the CEO of Design Group International, a Process Consulting Community of Practice. With his professional experience in organizational development, strategic planning, and institutional advancement, Lon's passion is to help leaders articulate vision, build consensus, obtain funding, and engage true and lasting change.

NICOLE TERRY, M.A.Ed., has over 25 years of experience working in education, consulting, and project management. She has dedicated the last 15 years to supporting American Indian/Alaska Native early childhood programs across the nation.

LILIAN VERNYUY, MS, APC, is a Nun of the Roman Catholic Church. Part of the Congregation of the Sisters of Saint Therese of the Child Jesus of Buea in Cameroon, she currently works as a Human Resource manager and General Supervisor while nursing a group of ninety-eight elderly people in Spain.

ABOUT THE AUTHOR

MARK L. VINCENT'S career is marked by innovations in executive leadership and organizational capacity development, His focus on helping organizations and leaders achieve mission objectives led to successful initiatives with more than 800 clients in varied domestic and international marketplaces. In 2000, he launched Design Group International, a Community of Practice for Process Consultants. In 2017, his brainstorming led to the establishment of the Society for Process Consulting.

Dr. Vincent's academic work included research into complex decision-making as well as economic strategy for associational systems (e.g., franchises, professional associations, denominations). He has written and presented extensively on stewardship and steward leader theology and practice, most notably *A Christian View of Money*. Mark's wife, Lorie, prior to her death at the end of a sixteen-year journey with leiomyosarcoma, joined him in writing the book *Fighting Disease, Not Death: Finding a Way Through Lifelong Struggle*. Mark later wrote the curated blog *Walking Beside my Dying Wife*, about his journey toward hope beyond the years of her suffering.

In addition to guiding classroom experiences for the Society for Process Consulting, Mark facilitates Maestro-level leader cohorts for seasoned executives focused on their firm's future value, cohosts *The Third Turn Podcast* with Kristin Evenson, and continues to assist the design of process to address unique and complex scenarios. The largest chunk of his professional life is given to sitting with seasoned executives and their boards as an Executive Advisor. Married to Patricia Teall Vincent, a coach and researcher, their time divides between family, work, and imaginative conversations in the various coffee shops of Boise, Idaho, and Eastern Wisconsin.

ACKNOWLEDGMENTS

I offer my deep appreciation and thanks to these key people and groups, without whom this work could not have been completed.

The Clients with whom I'm privileged to walk. For more than three decades I've been invited to sit with C-Suite leaders and the boards of organizations as we listened, helped, and learned together. Working with more than 800 diverse organizations serving many marketplaces is a priceless gift.

The Design Group International Partners and all those who have been part of its Community of Practice. We especially honor our memories of Lorie Vincent, because without her the Process Consulting Community of Practice that is Design Group International could not have been possible. And thank you David S. Bell and Philip C. Bergey, who continue to bring life, energy, and friendship to me through the decades of our business partnership.

The Society for Process Consulting, especially Kim Stezala, CEO, who championed the need for this book and made it possible. A special shout out to Lon Swartzentruber, Design Group International's CEO, who recruited experienced Process Consulting practitioners when we launched the original Core Competencies curriculum.

All those I've walked with in Process Consulting Training available through the Society for Process Consulting, some of whom contributed Case Studies for this book. Each one of you helps me continue to hone my skills.

Carol Mason, Darren Stezala, and Hallie Knox for their invaluable help in proofreading this manuscript and offering feedback on everything from punctuation to ultimate goals and meaning.

Jim Galvin, a friend and long-time example of listening well in difficult situations. His belief in the value of this project bolstered our efforts.

Ed Schein, godfather to this field of Process Consulting. Reading him. Re-reading him. And reading him yet again is worth every moment.

Kristin Evenson, co-hosting our work with Maestro-level leaders and the Third Turn Podcast. You are fresh air and cool, clean water.

Patricia Teall Vincent, my friend, confidante, and partner in life. As my daughter said to you: "You brought my Dad back to life."

ADDITIONAL RESOURCES

For more purchasing options and information on the book,
visit the publisher at www.tenthpowerpublishing.com.

For more information about the author
and the Society for Process Consulting,
visit www.societyforprocessconsulting.com.

Made in the USA
Monee, IL
05 August 2022

4f7707e2-432e-4500-87aa-823bd0dbe7a3R01